WATCHING RACEHORSES

Geoffrey Hutson was born and bred in Melbourne.

He spent over 20 years at the University of Melbourne as a Research Fellow in Animal Behaviour, studying the behaviour of a wide range of domestic animals, including sheep, cattle, pigs and horses.

He has written numerous articles for scientific journals, newspapers and magazines, including *Applied Animal Behaviour Science*, *New Scientist*, *The Age*, *The Sunday Age*, and *Turf Monthly* magazine. This is his first book.

He is now a full-time punter. He bets on the stockmarket for serious money and on racehorses for serious fun.

Good punting!

Geoffrey Hutson

WATCHING RACEHORSES

A GUIDE TO BETTING ON BEHAVIOUR

Geoffrey Hutson

CLIFTON PRESS

Published 2002 by Clifton Press
P.O. Box 1325, Kensington, Victoria, 3031
Fax: 03 9376 5912
Internet: www.watchingracehorses.com.au

National Library of Australia Cataloguing-in-Publication data:

Hutson, Geoffrey, 1947- .
Watching racehorses: a guide to betting on behaviour.

Bibliography.
Includes index.
ISBN 0 9581245 0 7.

1. Horse racing - Betting. 2. Race horses - Behavior.

798.401

Cover photograph by John Mole
Cover design by Liz Vagg
Printed in Australia by McPherson's Printing Group

Dedication

For my father,
Medwyn Hutson,
Who hardly had a bet in his life,
And my mother,
Patricia Wellington,
Who inadvertently gave me the gene.

Acknowledgements

Some of the ideas in this book were first expressed in articles written for *Turf Monthly* magazine, *The Age*, and Ausrace, an Internet horse racing discussion group. I am most grateful to Phil Rogers, Peter Schumpeter and Doug Robb for the opportunity to present my views on horse behaviour and punting in those forums.

Many thanks to the ethologists and horse scientists who have patiently answered my queries: Jonathon Cooper, University of Lincoln; Patricia Ellis, Victorian Institute of Animal Science; David Evans, University of Sydney; Alison Harman, University of Western Australia; Ocean Hartrick, Massey University; Marthe Kiley-Worthington, University of Exeter; Sue McDonnell, University of Pennsylvania; Finola McConaghy, University of Sydney; Paul McGreevy, University of Sydney; Robert Miller, retired US veterinarian; and Frank Ödberg, University of Ghent.

For permission to reproduce material I am indebted to: W.H. Freeman for Figure 2.1, General conformation and points of the horse; the Equine Veterinary Journal, for Figure 2.2, Body areas emphasised in condition scoring of horses by Don Henneke; the Victorian Department of Natural Resources and Environment for Figure 2.3, Condition scoring of horses by Lex Carroll and Peter Huntington; Elsevier Science, for Figure 3.1, Comparison of tail elevation and totalisator win dividend according to finishing position; The American Quarter Horse Journal for Figure 7.1, Types of snaffle bits; and W.B. Saunders for Figure 9.1, Some conformational faults in the fore and hind limbs of horses.

For photographs I am indebted to: J & J Digital Photographics, for the cover photo; Betsa Hutson for Photo 1, Bart and Geoffrey; Jenny Chandler for Photo 3, Van Der Hum and Geoffrey; Michael Silver, for Photo 4, Phar Lap and Geoffrey; the Powerhouse Museum for Photo 57, The George Julius model totalisator; and *The Age* for

Photo 58, John Singleton and wife in mounting yard. All other photographs were taken by the author.

Finally, thanks to all who have contributed towards improvement of the book, either directly through reading drafts and providing criticism, or indirectly, through providing information, stimulation, comment or discussion, especially Stephen Alomes, Slade Burnet, Matthew Connell, Paul Daffey, Betsa Hutson (The Missus), Bruce Hutson, John Hutson, Kate Hutson, E.J. Minnis (The Puntmaster), John Mole, Liz Vagg and Barbara Ward. And special thanks to two people: George Skarbek, who knows the answer to any question about the meaning of the computing universe, and Catherine Jones, my invaluable editor. It is a pleasure to note that any faults that remain in this book are mine alone. I feel like my school art teacher, who said when describing his own painting, "at least if it's awful, it's my kind of awful".

Table of contents

Introduction

I am a punter.

I admit it. And whenever I admit it, I usually find myself dragged before the Spanish Inquisition. Perhaps you are familiar with this experience? The three big questions: How much do you bet? Do you win? And, what's your system? As you can imagine, a punter tends to get fairly defensive when subjected to intensive interrogation, so I've developed reflex answers to these questions. Oh, well, I suppose about $200 a week. Yeah, well, I probably break even, but I've had a bit of a rough trot lately, and maybe I'm a little bit down, just at the moment. And, it's a secret.

So you can see, I'm just an average punter. I'm not a $1 each-way punter, and I'm not a $1000 on-the-nose high roller. Like most average punters, I'm also good at lying to others and fooling myself. Sure, I guess it's more like $500 a week, maybe more during the Spring Carnival. Average punters like me turn over between $20,000 and $50,000 a year. And, because I'm also a mildly obsessive and compulsive punter I know exactly whether I'm winning or losing because I've kept meticulous records and have written down every bet I've ever made since 1972. And my system? Well, it's still a secret. But let me tell you about it!

Like most punters, my betting life began with a ticket in a Melbourne Cup sweep. Third form, 1961. My sixpence drew Dhaulagiri out of the hat and returned two shillings and sixpence for third. Enough for three lime spiders at the tuck shop, and some change. I was hooked for life.

I progressed from this humble beginning through The Seven Ages of Punting Man. The First Age was seat of the pants punter, scanning the form guide, reacting to tips and coat tugs, listening to radio and newspaper experts, and losing. The Second Age was form student, avidly reading *The Sportsman*, and betting and losing in an informed manner. Even though I lost, I loved being regarded as a sportsman, without having to do any strenuous physical activity or put up with sweaty socks and jocks. The Third Age was serious, objective punter. I amassed a large database. Shoeboxes full of card records of the performance of every horse running around. Thousands of cards. A dynamic database before databases had been invented. I lost serious money. I decided it was time to become a post-graduate student of punting. I read everything I could lay my hands on. Rem Plante, Don Scott, Andy Beyer. I entered the Fourth, Fifth and Sixth Ages as a computer rater, using at first weights, then times, and finally class. The Seventh and final Age of Punting Man is where I am now. All previous ages have been relegated to the Stone Age and I now simply bet on what I see. I am now a fun punter, Spring Carnival enthusiast, and partygoer.

During the Sixth Age I had a lucky win and so I set up a gambling bank, putting it all into Tabcorp shares. As The Missus keeps reminding me, I now have a bigger bank than I would ever have had from betting on horses. And regardless of whether my horses win or lose, this bank grows inexorably bigger.

My main regret during my passage through the Punting Dark Ages was that I didn't know anything about horses. I had studied zoology at the university and specialised in animal behaviour. So I knew a bit about animals. I did an Honours study of bird song, a PhD on the behaviour of the Kowari, one of those nifty carnivorous marsupials, followed by a post-doctoral study on the behaviour of seagulls in the UK. On returning to Australia I found that there were no jobs for professional bird watchers so I worked on the behaviour of domestic animals - I watched sheep, and then cattle and pigs.

I was entering my Sixth Age in 1989 when a Kiwi student, Marie Haskell, came to do a PhD with me at Melbourne University on the behaviour of pigs. Marie turned up with a backpack on one shoulder and a saddle on the other. She was a riding instructor! At the first opportunity I spirited her off to the races. The rest, as they say in the classics, is history. We spent 20 months, off and on, looking at the horses. And then I spent another five years, mostly nights, analysing the data. Our paper "Pre-race behaviour of horses as a predictor of race finishing order" was finally published in the scientific journal *Applied Animal Behaviour Science* in 1997. We were famous.

In June 1997 I discarded the form guide forever. And with it came the realisation that I had spent some 25 years hanging around in racecourse bars and totes. I now attend the races with only a biro, a race book, sunscreen and hat. I spend most of Saturday afternoon outdoors, observing horses. I walk between 8 and 10 kilometres. My health and fitness is much improved. My liver has a new lease on life.

In June 1998 I gave up work at Melbourne University and became a full-time punter. Hey, don't get me wrong. I was retrenched. And I bet on the stock market for serious money. I bet on racehorses for serious fun.

This book contains pretty much everything I have learnt over the last 13 years of watching horses. It is intended to be a guide to the horses for all racegoers, regardless of their commitment to the punt. It is written for fun lovers; flutterers; Spring Carnival partygoers; regular, week-in, week-out punters; once-a-year wonders; big, hairy-chested punters; professional punters; owners; trainers; and people who simply just love horses. It is intended to be a guide for those who have tried any betting system, be it the pin method, lucky numbers, horse names, or jockey colours, and have experienced disappointment. In other words, it is intended for the 95 to 99% of people who have had a bet on a horse and lost. Quite clearly, it is time to have a closer look at the beast that carried your hard-earned to oblivion.

Chapter 1 describes a typical day at the races for a horse watcher, race by race. It is intended to get you into the mood of the book and give you a feel for life as a horse watcher. Chapters 2 and 3 explain how it all started and describe the initial scientific study of pre-race behaviour that I did with my student, Marie Haskell. In Chapter 2 I introduce the original variables we recorded and in Chapter 3 I outline the main results of the study. Chapter 4, Fifteen Minutes of Fame, describes the media feeding frenzy that followed publication of the results of this study in *New Scientist* magazine. Serious punters, keen to get to the nitty-gritty, can easily skip this chapter, with its self-indulgent descriptions of life in the fast lane.

Chapter 5, Picking Losers, returns to earth, and discusses the main reasons put forward for horses losing. I've tried to keep this chapter short, although it would be quite easy to devote several volumes to this topic.

Chapters 6 to 10 are the guts of the book. They describe in some detail what I now look at in the birdcage stalls, the parade ring, the mounting yard, and when horses are on the track.

Chapter 11 describes the results of an analysis of the 60 variables described in Chapters 6 to 10, based on observation of over 10,000 horses. This is the first time in horse racing history that actual statistics on the effect of behaviour on horse performance have been published. Chapter 12, Betting on Behaviour, proposes a few ideas for betting on the results of horse watching, including betting for the win and making a Dutch book. Chapter 13, Which Horse, Which Race? points out what types of horse and what types of race are most suitable for betting on behaviour. Chapter 14 describes some of the practical difficulties of applying horse watching techniques to our most famous race, the Melbourne Cup. And finally, Further Reading provides a comprehensive bibliography of all references cited throughout the book.

Most people say that they would like to look at the horses, but don't know where to look. This book shows you where, and how. No knowledge of form, form guides, racing slang, breeding, mathematics or astrology is required. All you need is a pen, the race book, and your peepers. Let's watch racehorses!

Chapter 1 A day at the races

I think I've got throat cancer. The GP has a look but can't see anything. He looks at his records and sees that I've been complaining about it for nearly a year now. Time to do something. So I'm off to the specialist. A bit worrying really, wondering if you're for it. I try to imagine what it will be like to be dead. Kerry Packer's quote comes to mind: "I've been there, and let me tell you, son. There's fucking nothing there". The Fitzroy Gardens in a Melbourne winter are an appropriate place to linger outside Outpatients and contemplate oblivion. Dank, cold, and the Fairy Tree is just a dead old tree stump.

The specialist sprays some anaesthetic down, but the throat keeps gagging up when he pokes his stick in. I'm for the high chair. This is another room, subdued lighting, dominated by a central red leather high chair. It reminds me of a sado-masochist's parlor. Not that I'd know. I think of Laurence Olivier in the *Marathon Man* and his drill. More anaesthetic, this time up the nose, and he produces The Black Snake. He commands me to relax, which I try to do, but with some difficulty. The Snake goes up my nose, does a U-turn, and then dives down into my throat. I just keep my eyes tightly shut, concentrating on breathing. I surprise myself by coping. Say "Eeeeeeeeeeeee". I'm "Eeeeeeeeeing" like crazy. An eternity, and The Snake's finally had enough. "Well, it looks fine to me".

A surge of relief as I stagger out into the gardens. Suddenly I notice that the sun is out, trees are exploding into leaf, flowers are blooming, birds are singing. The Fairy Tree is alive with coloured gnomes and elves crawling all over it. I remember this is where Auntie Dix brought us as kids. It was magic, then. It is magic, now. Ah, isn't it great. To be alive. Spring! Bring on the races. I'm bursting for a bet.

Race 1. Craiglee Stakes, Flemington, 9 September 2000

I'm off in my best clobber to Girls Day Out, the first day of the new season. I have two goals. First, to check out my new VRC Members' card, and second, to have a good squiz at Streak. He looked so good that I gasped when I last saw him in the autumn, first-up, powering home for third in the Carlyon Cup.

I've joined the toffs because I'm getting old. Silvertail membership means that my trek from stables to parade ring to mounting yard to bookies or tote is shortened by some 200 metres. All up, 1.6 kilometres a day, a not inconsiderable saving for an older person. I plunge the card into the slot, and ping, I'm in. They let anyone in these days. I can now discard my pocket full of old Members' visitor passes, which I've kept for over 10 years. Before they had barcodes, you could always find an old one that matched the shape and colour of today's ticket.

In the stand a matron with a fur coat is telling everyone how she hit a young man on the shoulder with her umbrella when he wouldn't sit down. He'd had too much to drink, of course. He turned around menacingly and she thought he was going to punch her lights out. Really! She complains that the Members is not like it used to be. They let anyone in these days. Hear, hear. I make a mental note to nominate my favourite footballer, Dean Wallis, for life membership.

I narrow the Craiglee down to Umrum, Oliver Twist, Go Flash Go and Ad Alta. Go Flash Go is fit and Ollie is a fighter. Ad Alta collapses and drops dead on the turn out of the straight. A horse watcher remarks to me, after the race of course, that he put a cross next to it, because it was showing some white eye in the parade ring. I congratulated him. It must be the first time he's picked a dead 'un before the race! I can't say I've ever done that.

But it's the race after the Craiglee I've come for, a 1400 metre listed sprint. The cold and wet precludes my usual trek to the stables. They arrive in the yard with their coats on. "Mount up please riders". But I haven't even seen Streak naked! My mobile rings. It's The Missus with urgent gossip. I hang up, look up, and they're gone. I ask the wise old head next to me if he saw Streak without his coat and he said he looked very good. But, no see, no bet. Streak, as expected, powers home.

Race 2. Turnbull Stakes, Flemington, 7 October 2000

I'm clutching my silver invitation from The Chairman to a pre-race party at silvertail headquarters. It's meant to be a soft opening of the new grandstand, whatever that means, and I have to get there an hour early, for the free grog. I'm on the escalators and by sheer chance The Chairman is right in front of me. But he gets off at the third level, The Chairman's Club. He's not even going to his own party! He's got his own private club!

I was expecting just a few die-hard punters prepared to drink at 11.30 am, but hey, there's about 5000 here. How many champagnes can you drink in one hour? My first goes down in a flash. Number two, and I look around for Tatiana. Can't see her anywhere. You'll remember the Spring Carnival was officially launched by the three stars, Subzero, my last cup winner, Vintage Crop, the Irish wonder horse, and Tatiana "show me the money" Grigorieva, pole vaulter and Olympic silver medallist. Did you see Tatiana on TV, or that photo in the paper of her red dress, or that soft-porn magazine cover with the tattoos? For the face of the spring carnival, she's sure showing a lot of body. All muscle, tendon and sinew. I'm keen to see her in the flesh and try out a "show us yer tatt". Third champers. She's playing hard to get, nowhere to be seen. Maybe I'd better settle. Time for a quiet champagne to look at the new facilities. Stunning city views, but still not as good a view of the post as from the Hill Stand. Better have a drink to watch the drizzle. A thought. Champagne PLUS rain EQUALS danger. I find myself standing next to Bart Cummings, trying out some new binoculars on the big screen.

I brush against him for good luck. Steady, old fella. He puts the binos down, and it's not Bart at all. Just a regular silvertail. I look around and realise that half the blokes here look like Bart, well provisioned, slicked-back silver hair. The whole stand is now abuzz. Smart cookies are lining them up, stockpiling. It must be nearly 12.30. Time for one for the road.

And the answer? Five and a half. Thank goodness it wasn't a hard opening. I need a good sit down. I know I should look at the horses, but they move in and out of focus. The fourth race, and finally I have regained enough conscious thought to have a gander. But it's too hard, no bet. Back to my patch, the birdcage, to check out the unveiling of Bart's statue. The Labor Party hard man and Minister for Racing, Rob Hulls, is doing the honours. He remarks to Bart "I hope it bloody well looks like you". But first Shane Bourne, the comedian, is going to read a poem by "Barry from the bush". He can't resist the one-liners, Shane. He's 51 years old now. "Being good in bed means you don't hog the doona". Fifteen verses. And the last verse:

> And drink to one whose prowess
> Has made him known to all,
> A man who walks amongst us
> Admired and standing tall,
> A man of fame and modesty,
> Our favorite every start,
> A man who trumped adversity,
> Drink one and all to Bart.

Did someone say drink? Suddenly there's more free champagne and Bart is looking all misty-eyed and posing for photos with his likeness (Photo 1). Not too bad, either. But he can keep his 11 Cups. I've had six and a half glasses.

All this partying and I've missed the fifth race. I've only got two rules when I go to the races. Never drink and never bet on horses you haven't seen. So I have my first bet for the day, a small place wager

Photo 1
Bart and Geoffrey.

on Citra's Prince in the Metropolitan Handicap in Sydney, sight unseen. Was stunningly fit when last scrutinised at Moonee Valley in the Feehan Stakes. Snatches third at $5.90. Whew! I vow never, ever to do that again.

And finally, the Turnbull. Oliver Twist, my main betting intention, is still in his stall. Most unusual. Looks OK to me, slightly more agitated than usual, but hand-held, nibbling the tie-up. The siren, and Ollie comes out with an abnormality in his pre-race blood test. What's up? Was he got at? I have an unconvincing bet on Streak, who runs an unconvincing sixth. I feel like I've been got at. I think I'm getting a headache. The Missus reckons I'm a hypochondriac.

Race 3. Caulfield Guineas, 9 October 1999

Guineas day. How could I ever forget this day in 1972. I backed Century, and was nutted by the mighty Sobar. But that's not what I remember. I got something in my eye, and my brother John, learning how to be a doctor, got out a matchstick to roll my eyelid back, and I clear passed out, in a dead faint, unconscious, on the floor of the Guineas Stand. I'll have to watch it, today.

I've come, of course, to have a big bet on Redoute's Choice, a fabulous horse. I've backed him at each start so far. His last run at Flemington was a disaster. The rain was the worst I can remember for some time. I had to stop betting after the third because my race book became so soggy that I couldn't make notes in it. I walked the length of the straight, criss-crossing it on the way home, and you could only describe it as greasy, greasy. Plenty of excuses for a good horse.

The two champions are in the parade ring. Testa Rossa with a tongue tie, a minor worry, but not too serious since he's won with it before. He baulks going up to the yard, also a minor worry. Redoute's Choice looks fine. But whoa! What's that! A fabulous colt, a standout in any other race. Commands! I see that I've already written in my race book that he was hand-held in the stall. That's a good sign, and here's the strapper still stroking him. Positive strapper is a big plus! My carefully laid plans of a big bet on Redoute's Choice are thrown into instant confusion. I rush up to the yard. Redoute's Choice is not totally relaxed.

What to do? Suddenly there is a thunderclap and a blinding light. My eyelid rolls back and I feel like I'm falling. I have a vision, and the misty form of an old man appears. Is it my brother? Is it Moses? Whoever, he's an old bugger, and carrying a large stone tablet, which has one word engraved upon it - "PLACE". But, but Moses, I never bet the place! But, but it's hard to argue with a stone tablet. I'm barely conscious, battling to get to the tote window. My big bet goes onto Commands for the place.

The two champions come pounding down the straight. The crowd is bringing the stand down with their cheering for the match race. But did you hear me? Did anyone hear me? Moses? Go Commands! Go you good thing! $8.40 for third!

Race 4. Caulfield Cup, 17 October 1998

As I stride into Caulfield racecourse I'm besieged by giants on stilts, Fosters and Optus girls in skimpy, shape-hugging outfits, and freebies galore. A basket of condoms is thrust towards me. The VATC giving away condoms? A bit optimistic for some of us, don't you think? She laughs, and they turn out to be little packets of breath freshener. I guess the club is getting tired of all the bad-mouthing they've been copping.

It's a bad day for horse watchers. A gale force northerly wind is playing havoc with hair, hats and frocks. And the horses, they hate it. Lots of dust in the air. The ears, that reliable window to the horse's soul, are totally unreliable. Each horse has them pinned back heading north up the parade ring, then nicely pricked heading south.

The overseas horses are stabled in a corner up the back. I keep going to check up on them. At last Taufan's Melody arrives. My first glimpse is a big disappointment. He's got a bloody great big nose roll. A fairly ordinary looking horse, ordinary coat, but relaxed. Your typical B-grade pommy stayer. How I hate nose rolls. You could count the number of long shot winners with nose rolls on an amputee's hand. He hates the wind, even in his box, and the strapper turns him round, backside out. He's fit enough to win! My daughter, Ruth, turns up to have a look too, and the wind is so strong it blows the sauce from her hot dog onto her brand new hat. Dead horse on a hat will never do!

I return again after the fifth race and Faithful Son has now arrived. Again, my first sight is disappointing. Bandages! A fairly small, light type, and nice coat, nice blaze. But doesn't seem to have the build to survive the hurly-burly of a Caulfield Cup. And those bandages!

I'm back again after the sixth. What is it that brings me back to these horses? Lady Herries is saddling him up. By golly, she's the spitting image of Betty Windsor, just 10 sizes bigger. And a hat to match. She's struggling with the girth strap. Dare I say it? Her own is interfering with the procedure a bit. The horse kicks out and the lady gives him a slap. Taufan's Melody is first into the ring, just like Dane Ripper last year before she won the Plate. Nothing to lose, everything to gain. Looking around a bit, little bit head up. I put the pen through him. Two strikes and you're out - distracted and nose roll. Tie The Knot looks nice and he carries mine, with a saver on Faithful Son.

The rest as they say is history. Fayreform comes out at the gate, and we all yell out for the club to bring on the emergency, the unlucky Our Unicorn, eliminated at the committee's discretion. The B-grade stayer knocks them flying in the straight, but survives the protest. The stewards must have used their discretion, too.

Race 5. Moonee Valley Gold Cup, 22 October 1998

Night racing. This is my first time. Normally I'm not allowed out after dark. The fat giants on stilts are out again, in black suits and with bouncer ID numbers, guarding the entrance. My daughter K8 has warned me to keep away from the disco, Dad.

Straight to stall number one to check out the favourite. There's Colin Alderson on the mobile. Eavesdropping reveals a minor stable staffing problem. Our Unicorn looks OK, if unlucky horses ever can look OK. The connections are still spewing over not getting a run in the Caulfield Cup. Did you see its saddlecloth number? 13! Black cats!

So what's it like for a horse watcher? Well, there is no straw in the stalls at Moonee Valley which makes assessment of excreta easier, if you're into that sort of thing, but harder to see if they are pawing. And it's hard to read the horse name cards. The stalls are lit from behind which leaves the name in the dark. And if you are a fatness and fitness assessor like Roy Higgins, the Sport 927 mounting yard reporter, then it must be even harder because the shapes are all shadowed. The crowd is small, but enthusiastic, and there are many more young 'uns. Out on the lawn it's very impressive. Millions of moths cavorting in the grandstand lights, and below, thousands of punters, moths too, moths to the flame.

I seem to be the only person using binoculars. I soon see why - you can see bugger all at night. Best just to watch the races on the big screen. Soon it's time for the Hush Puppy Gold Cup. Colin Alderson is picking his teeth with his fingernails, a bad sign. The oriental owners seem inscrutable, but must be churning inside over the saddlecloth. Our Unicorn starts kicking the stall, not normally a good sign. But then Taufan's Melody let go one irritated kick, which earned him a slap, before winning the Caulfield Cup. Our Unicorn is not punished. Into the ring. His ears are back. I lick my finger and thrust it into the air. There is no gale force northerly wind. He is not entirely happy with himself. New Kingston has a nose roll. Now that's a new dimension. A nose roll under lights. Four horses have no faults - Second Coming, Skybeau, Brilliant Poet and Prince Standaan. I back them all. Second Coming gives a great sight, but the Prince stampedes home. Ah, the ironies of racing. The second Caulfield Cup emergency is the one that should have felt aggrieved.

Highlight of the night? I saw a lady tipster tip a scratching on the closed circuit TV. At least you wouldn't lose backing it!

Time to go home. Check out stall one. Our Unicorn is rugged and ready to go home too, but still kicking! They're queued up outside Cactus, the disco. But I remember my instructions. Anyway, it's after 10.30, and I'm well and truly cactus.

Race 6. Cox Plate, Moonee Valley, 25 October 1997

The programme is pathetic. Small fields, topped off with a Class 6. It's hot weather and hot work and I need a couple of races to figure out a strategy for looking at the horses, then getting a bet on, and then watching the race with a reasonable view. I have come mainly to have a bet on Spartacus in the sprint, and I also fancy the three-year-olds in the WFA race. Spartacus is already doing laps of the parade ring before the fifth race, and is sweating up.

First horse out for the Plate is Dane Ripper. No faults, just sweating a bit in the flank. Next out Tarnpir Lane, gait is a bit fast, with occasional tail flicks at the flies. Then a rush of them. The EnZedders. Moss Downs does something I don't like, and Vialli is head down, relaxed. Alfa, crossover noseband, don't like them, tail sometimes swished, sometimes stiff, sometimes relaxed. A problem horse. And there's Juggler. Can't win. Stiff tail, slight head up, chewing the ring bit, bit of sweat between the hind legs. Something wrong with him. Filante. Ace!! Encounter, looks OK, occasional tail flicking. Schubert. Fine. Chewing the ring bit. They head out to the mounting yard and I follow them down. There's a chain up across the yard. And Filante and Juggler who have already arrived are now sent back. They are going to introduce the jockeys over the PA in the mounting yard. I don't believe it - jockeys taking precedence over horses in the mounting yard for the Cox Plate? The horses come back to the parade ring and only a few of us follow them back. Everyone else has taken up a possie on the yard. Can you believe it! Ten minutes before the start of Australasia's greatest WFA race and I can literally touch and look at all the horses, and yet there's only a handful of people around! Encounter is getting very upset. The routine has been changed! He starts revolving his tail, head up, agitated. Rick Hore-Lacy comes over and stands next to me. I remark that Spartacus looks nice, but is sweating a bit. He's worried. He says the horse is hot. I suggest that it is a disgrace sending the horses back from the yard, but he reckons the horses are probably better off anyway, because it's cooler here. They finally go, and now I've ruled out Encounter, Moss Downs, Tarnpir Lane, Juggler. Query on Alfa. Decide to back Schubert. Get to the tote and notice on the TV Filante colliding with some pot plants! Unreal. Get to my race spot, and Filante's still not happy at the barrier. I'd get off him if I was on him! The rest is history. Dane Ripper slays them. Schubert's jockey should be shot.

Now the race I'm waiting for. Spartacus is still hot, but you can't rule them out on that alone. In the yard he suddenly flares up his tail as if to do an almighty dump, but then he doesn't. I watch Hore-Lacy. He's seen it and glances backward to look at the dump. There isn't one. But he's still looking worried. That was a very worried, sly, backward glance. I decide to back the next five horses in the betting market. Spartacus is definitely too hot!!

Race 7. Welter Handicap, Royal Randwick, 16 February 2002

I've come to Sydney to check out conditions for horse watchers, and you'd have to say, they are very demanding. I leave my comfortable lodgings at Artarmon at 11.45 am, one hour before the first. The train trip over the bridge is stunning, but the 372 bus to Coogee is a nightmare. The passengers comprise an unholy mixture of middle-aged male punters fanning themselves with form guides and curvaceous young women in bikinis heading off to the beach. It feels like 40 °C, and the humidity must be 85%. The bus seems to be stationary. Rivulets of sweat plunge down into the nether regions of the bikinis, and the punters look like boiled beetroots. It takes us over half an hour to battle across from Central Station to Anzac Parade. We're disgorged at Randwick, half alive, at 1.30 pm. They're about to jump in the second.

Quite clearly, considerable fluid intake will be required to eliminate my dehydration. By the sixth I'm just about stabilised and can look around. By golly, I'm totally surrounded by well-known Sydney racing identities. Hey, there's Bob, Singo, Gai, Robbie, Bill, Don,

Pumper, Billy, and Bossy. And is that Murray and George? Gosh, I hope it's safe here. There's good access to all the horse stalls, except for the bit where you have to walk around the parade ring. But, unlike Flemington, at least you can see all the horses. Following them up to the mounting yard is a bit harder as you have to run the gauntlet of dehydrated members and battle through a sea of plastic chairs and tables. The yard is a peculiar shape and the horses run the wrong way on the track, but I suppose you can get used to anything. At least the horses behave much the same. In the seventh I cross them all out except Cheverny, who duly salutes at $3.70 the place.

Queuing up for the dreaded bus home I'm accosted by two girls wielding large plastic penises. They squeeze the testicles and I'm squirted by jets of water. Ah hah, they are water pistols. And there is a mob of 15 beefy youths in khaki shorts and shirts and platinum blonde wigs. No doubt, a rugby club. But can the world cope with 15 Steve Irwins? Croc hunter clones? A large green plastic crocodile is thrown to the ground and one of them jumps on it and wrestles with it in a death roll. The crowd in the queue loves it. They then decide that I shouldn't be on the bus. I must be a professional punter, since I won, only had three bets, and didn't have a bet on the last. This bus is apparently reserved for desperates.

Sydney sure is different. I think it's like Cup Day, every day. But why is it Royal Randwick? I thought this was a republican town.

Race 8. Racing Legends Plate, Caulfield, 14 October 2000

It's the last race on Guineas Day, the get-out stakes, and I'm down the gurgler. But it's my favourite class of race, for mares four years and up. I love it how mares wear their hearts on their sleeves. I narrow it down to two horses. The favourite Crixia, who looks stunning, and a long shot, Heart of Egypt, with no faults. Crixia is showing $1.10 a place, so I back the 18, Heart of Egypt. A quick look at the race book for the colours, pink, and they're off. Crixia goes straight to the front with Heart of Egypt midfield. Crixia, as expected, has them struggling on the corner and kicks clear. But Pareto nails her on the line and my bet finishes midfield somewhere. Just like a long shot should. Oh well, I know I should put my pen away in the wet. They're coming back to scale. Number 18 is going in with the place getters. Must've finished fifth, and has to weigh in. Hey, but she's going in to the third stall. Hey, they weren't the pink colours I was following. I look up at the semaphore board. 11, 5, 18. Well, fancy that. I slap my knee. I look at the place odds on 18. $9.40! Another slap. You could knock me over with a feather. Isn't the Spring Carnival the greatest! I feel like Richard Dreyfuss in that B-movie *Let It Ride*. Suddenly, I have had a very good day. And how I love walking home with money in my shoes. Do you think I look taller?

Chapter 2 A little looksee

September 9, 1989. Indeed, it was a beautiful day, full of hope and the promise of infinite riches. The sun was streaming through the split windscreen of my Australian icon, the 1955 FJ Holden Special Sedan, as Marie and I tootled down Racecourse Road. We were feeling pretty perky, cocky even. After all, we were about to look at some horses and pick some winners. We'd spent some time back in the Animal Behaviour Laboratory at the University of Melbourne Farm, kicking around ideas for important variables, and we'd come up with an interim list of sorts. We thought that winners would look good and behave well, so we had included both appearance variables and behaviour variables in our list. Marie was scanning the form guide, reading out names. Some of the horses that raced that day would bring a tear to the eye of even hardened punters. Super Impose, Tawriffic, The Phantom, Sydeston.

I keep telling The Missus that it's hard work at the races. She has the impression that it's all champagne and chicken sandwiches, and I must say that watching horseflesh with young, nubile women, does sound quite agreeable. But we soon discovered the truth of Malcolm Fraser's truism. Life wasn't meant to be easy. To fully appreciate Malcolm's epigram you need to consider the pre-race routine and racecourse layout, which is much the same at most Australian racecourses. There is a 35-minute gap between most races, and the horses don't start to appear in public view until about 15 to 20 minutes before race time. The horses are led by their strappers from their stalls in the stable area, known as the birdcage, and may do two or three laps of the parade ring, before walking down the laneway to the mounting yard. Again, the horses may be led on one or two laps of the mounting yard before the trainer, jockey and owners appear in the yard and the jockey is legged up onto the horse by the trainer. The horses may then do another lap or two of the mounting yard before they are accompanied onto the track by two or three mounted clerks of the course. Once on the track, depending on the race distance, the horses may walk, trot or canter 200 metres or so down the track in the opposite direction from the barrier and then return at full speed in a warm-up gallop. The horses will then mingle behind the barrier until called forward by the official race starter into the stalls for the race start.

The maximum field size is 24 horses, and the minimum viewing time is about 15 minutes, which theoretically allows about 38 seconds to assess the condition, appearance and behaviour of each horse. We were recording 19 variables for each horse and so we found that in some races we were working under considerable time pressure, with only two or three seconds to score each variable. In addition, many trainers try to hold their horses back in the birdcage until the last minute, to minimise their exposure to the pre-race atmosphere and tension. Often we had to run to keep up with the late horses on their way to the mounting yard. At Flemington we reckoned we walked or ran up to 10 kilometres a day. We used to look forward to meetings at the more compact Moonee Valley. They were aerobically less demanding.

The variables were recorded on a check sheet, which I held on a clipboard. Marie would yell out what the horse looked like and I'd write it down. "Light type, good condition, good fitness, glossy coat, slight sweating, gentle hold, 30 centimetre strap. Head, ears, tail all OK". I scribbled furiously. Run after the next one. Puff, puff. "Good type, fat, poor fitness, poor coat, firm hold, zero strap". Run, puff, run. "Light type, good, good, firm hold, 20 strap, head up, unsettled gait". Run, run. "Damn, missed it". Punters carrying clipboards on a racecourse are regarded as serious students of form and therefore we were generally ignored by the public or regarded with only slight bemusement. Those who were interested in what we were doing were usually satisfied with the explanation that "it's a student project".

We did this off and on for 20 months. More off than on, for reasons which will soon become apparent. We only worked if the track condition was rated as good or fast, or in other words, unaffected by rain. Overall, we attended 10 race meetings, five at Moonee Valley and five at Flemington. We looked at 867 horses entered in 69 flat races. Here's our list of variables:

Table 2.1
The looksee list of 19 variables

Variable	Score
Horse type	Rangy, light, good, stocky
Fatness	Thin, thin/good, good, good/fat, fat
Fitness	Poor, medium, good, excellent
Coat condition	Poor, normal, glossy
Sweating	None, slight, medium, heavy
Blinkers	Recorded if present
Bandages	Recorded if present
Strapper hold	Gentle, firm
Strap length	Estimated to nearest 5 centimetres
Head position	Down, normal, up
Ear position	Forwards, sideways, disinterested, back
Tail position	Relaxed, stiff, swished
Speed of gait	Normal, fast
Arousal	Normal, unsettled head, unsettled gait, bucking
Head position - jockey up	Down, normal, up
Neck angle - jockey up	Down, normal, up
Resistance to bit	Mouth closed, mouth open, resisting
Led by clerk	Recorded if grabbed by clerk
Tracking	Recorded if cantering or galloping sideways on track

We concentrated on variables that those grizzled old geezers hanging over the mounting yard fence look at. Things such as fatness, fitness, coat condition and sweating. But immediately, we were confronted with the first problem facing apprentice horse watchers. Where do you look? Well, I'd suggest that the best place to look, first up, is at the horse in Figure 2.1.

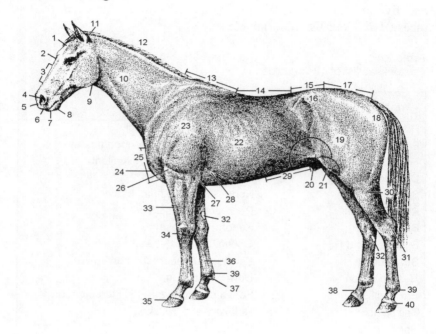

1	Forehead	11	Poll	21	Stifle	31	Hock
2	Face	12	Crest	22	Barrel	32	Chestnut
3	Bridge of nose	13	Withers	23	Shoulder	33	Forearm
4	Nostril	14	Back	24	Point of shoulder	34	Knee
5	Muzzle	15	Loin	25	Chest	35	Hoof
6	Upper lip	16	Point of hip	26	Arm	36	Cannon
7	Lower lip	17	Croup	27	Elbow	37	Ergot
8	Under lip	18	Buttock	28	Girth	38	Pastern
9	Throat latch	19	Thigh	29	Abdomen	39	Fetlock
10	Neck	20	Flank	30	Gaskin	40	Coronet

Figure 2.1
General conformation and points of the horse.
Reprinted from J.W. Evans, A. Borton, H.F. Hintz, and L.D. van Vleck, The Horse, 1977, by permission of the publisher, W.H. Freeman.

It is well worthwhile devoting a few minutes to this figure. Before starting to look a horse watcher really does need to know the names of all the different body bits of a horse. You have to be able to sort out a crest from a croup, a gaskin from a girth, a hock from a fetlock. I will be referring to these various horse parts throughout this book, so careful study of Figure 2.1 will pay off. As a test, find the ergot, the chestnut and the throat latch. A side benefit of careful study will be the ability to impress friends and anyone else within earshot with comments such as "That one looks a bit weak in the stifle" or "There's a dodgy gaskin".

The first thing that Marie and I looked at was the general conformation of the horse, which is what the aforementioned mounting yard geezers mean when they say "That's a nice type". Horses come in all sorts of shapes and sizes. So our first variable, **Horse type**, was a simple attempt to classify shape and size. We scored horses as either *Rangy* - if they looked skinny, spindly or narrow; *Light* - if they looked light-boned, but of reasonable conformation; *Good* - if they were a well-proportioned horse; or *Stocky* - if they were a well-built, strong-boned horse. We didn't really expect horse type to be much of a predictor of performance, but it did help us to get our eyes used to looking at and evaluating the conformation of different horses.

Next, we thought that we should score **Fatness** or body condition by visual appraisal of areas likely to indicate changes in stored fat. But what and where are those areas? Fortunately, we found a paper by Don Henneke at Tarleton State University, Texas, who had developed a nine category scoring system for condition scoring horses. Don's system focused on six areas of the horse (*see* Figure 2.2): the ribs, withers, neck, the area behind the shoulder, the crease down the backbone, and the tailhead. A horse with a score of 1 was extremely emaciated and a horse with a score of 9 was extremely fat.

We used a similar system, but since extremely thin and extremely fat horses are not seen on the racecourse, we needed only five categories.

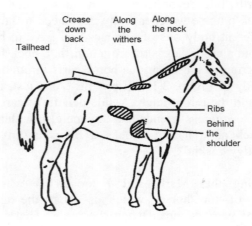

Figure 2.2
Body areas assessed in condition scoring of horses by Don Henneke.
Reprinted from D.R.Henneke, G.D. Potter, J.L. Kreider and B.F. Yeates,
Relationship between condition score, physical measurements and body fat
percentage in mares, 1983, Equine Veterinary Journal 15, 371-2, with
permission of the publisher.

We scored horses as *Thin* - if the horse looked "ribby" and the
backbone, croup and tailhead were prominent; *Good* - if the horse
was well-covered, and the ribs could not be individually
distinguished, the neck was firm and the backbone was well-covered;
or *Fat* - if the horse was carrying surplus condition, especially on the
stomach, along the withers and neck, and behind the shoulders. The
ribs were not visible and often there was a crease running along the
back. We also scored the intermediate categories *Good/Thin* and
Fat/Good, so that our resulting five categories were equivalent to Don
Henneke's categories of Thin (3) through to Fleshy (7).

Other horse watchers may use other slightly different scales for
condition scoring. For example, Patricia Ellis at the Victorian
Department of Natural Resources and Environment uses the six

category system developed by Lex Carroll and Peter Huntington. The categories range from 0 (Very Poor) through to 5 (Very Fat). I've shown the four categories most likely to be seen in racehorses in Figure 2.3.

Poor horses will never be seen at a racetrack, but Poor/Moderate (1/2) horses, which are equivalent to our category of *Thin*, are encountered now and then. The average condition score of a racehorse is between Moderate and Good (equivalent to 5 on Don Henneke's scale and our category of *Good*). Patricia's diagrams are worth a close inspection and illustrate quite clearly the changes in appearance as a horse puts on or loses condition.

Scoring body condition takes practice. And then more practice. It's even better if you can get your hands on a horse or a hack to palpate the different areas and get a feel for different amounts of fat covering on the pelvis, rump, back, ribs and neck.

Fitness is also hard, if not impossible to measure, simply by looking at a horse. When people talk about fitness, they generally mean aerobic fitness. This can include the ability of the lungs to supply oxygen to the blood, the ability of the heart to move blood to the muscles, and the ability of the muscles to use the oxygen for athletic performance. Fitness can also include the ability of the muscles to produce energy without oxygen, also known as anaerobic fitness. Aerobic and anaerobic fitness will respond to training so that a horse's performance will improve. Most improvements in aerobic fitness occur over a 6-8 week period after the start of training. To measure these improvements we really need to call in an equine exercise physiologist, such as David Evans, at the University of Sydney. To measure fitness David uses a treadmill and very expensive equipment for gas analysis. His main measure is the maximum oxygen uptake at different speeds on the treadmill until the horse is fatigued. Heart rate is another useful measure of fitness, and heart rate recovery following exercise is routinely used to assess fitness in endurance horses. Lactic acid concentration in the blood is

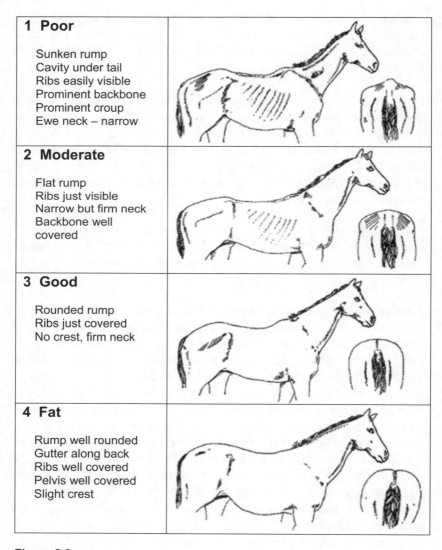

1 Poor

Sunken rump
Cavity under tail
Ribs easily visible
Prominent backbone
Prominent croup
Ewe neck – narrow

2 Moderate

Flat rump
Ribs just visible
Narrow but firm neck
Backbone well
covered

3 Good

Rounded rump
Ribs just covered
No crest, firm neck

4 Fat

Rump well rounded
Gutter along back
Ribs well covered
Pelvis well covered
Slight crest

Figure 2.3
Condition scoring of horses by Lex Carroll and Peter Huntington.
Reprinted from Patricia Ellis, Condition scoring and weight estimation of horses, Agriculture Note AG0928, © The State of Victoria, Department of Natural Resources and Environment, 2000.

another useful measure of fitness, with superior horses generally having lower blood lactate concentrations after exercise. If you are seriously into horses as an owner or trainer then David's booklet on *Training and Fitness in Athletic Horses* is well worth a read. However, for casual racegoers and party animals it's not worth getting too hung up on fitness. Simply accept that we can't take a treadmill to the track or readily get our hands on a blood sample.

Marie and I decided that we would score fitness simply by looking at the definition of some of the muscles in the hindquarters, which should give us an indirect measure of the amount of training a horse has had. It's a bit like looking at Steve Moneghetti, the marathon runner, and assessing his body fat condition by looking at his stomach and then assessing his fitness by looking at the development and definition of his thigh or calf muscles. We looked at muscle groups in the upper gaskin and lower thigh, as viewed from the rear, with the horse walking away from us. These muscles form the hamstring group of muscles - the biceps femoris, the semitendonosus and the semimembranosus, and are involved in propelling the horse forward. We mainly looked at the semitendinosus and the three divisions of the biceps femoris (*see* Photo 2).

Four levels of fitness were scored, based solely on the amount of definition of these muscle groups. *Poor* fitness was recorded if there was poor or no definition of all muscle groups; *Medium* fitness if a groove between the semitendinosus and biceps, known as the "poverty line", was visible and there was vague definition of other groups; *Good* fitness if the poverty line was visible, there were clear creases outlining one of the divisions of the biceps femoris, and less clear definition of the second group; and *Excellent* fitness if there was a pronounced poverty line, and clear definition of two divisions of the biceps femoris muscle. In *Good* and *Excellent* horses a crease running roughly parallel to the poverty line, between the semimembranosus and the semitendinosus, was also usually visible.

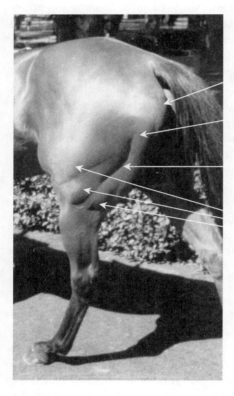

Semimembranosus
muscle

Semitendinosus
muscle

Poverty line

Biceps femoris muscle –
three divisions

Photo 2
Hindquarters of Crixia, Moonee Valley, 23 March 2002.
The three main muscles of the hamstring group are shown.

Most mounting yard observers look at **Coat condition**, and so we did too. We scored it according to the fineness of the hair covering, which indicates the presence of the summer coat, and also its sleekness, or the degree to which it lies close to the skin surface. Coat condition was recorded as *Poor* - if the coat looked dull, or the hair was coarse, or was "turned up"; *Normal* - if the coat looked like a normal bright coat; or *Glossy* - if the coat was vibrant, sleek, and shining. Some horse watchers regard dappling of the coat as an important variable and an indicator of good health. We didn't record dappling, as it seems only to be associated with particular coat colours, in particular grey and bay.

Sweating is generally pretty obvious to most horse watchers and we scored it by visual appraisal of the areas where horses sweat most readily - at the base of the ears and on the neck, chest, and flanks. Sweating was recorded as *None*; *Slight* - if small patches of sweat were visible, e.g. under the saddlery; *Medium* - if larger patches were visible under the saddlery, or small patches were showing in the flank, chest or neck; or *Heavy* - if large areas were affected or there were signs of lather.

We also noted whether the horse carried any special gear such as **Blinkers** or **Bandages**, which included both "tapes", light bandages on the horse's bumpers (remember those ergots?), or larger bandages, commonly protecting the horse's shin or cannon bone.

With our remaining variables we concentrated on the behaviour of the horse in the parade ring and mounting yard. We were interested in how much effort the strapper needed to exert to control the horse so we scored **Strapper hold,** as *Gentle* or *Firm*, and **Strap length**, which was a guesstimate to the nearest 5 cm of the length of the leading strap between the strapper's hand and the horse's bit. We also noted how the horse was carrying its **Head**, **Ears** and **Tail** as it was led by the strapper, the speed of its **Gait**, and its general **Arousal**. I'll discuss these variables in more detail in Chapter 9.

We checked the behaviour of the horse again once the jockey was up in the saddle. We scored both **Head** and **Neck position,** and **Resistance to the bit.** Resistance was recorded as *Mouth Closed* - if the mouth was closed around bit; *Mouth Open* - if the mouth was open around bit, but the horse was not apparently pulling against it; or *Resisting* - if the mouth was open around bit and the horse was apparently pulling against the bit. If a clerk of the course grabbed hold of the reins or bridle of a horse we recorded this as **Led by clerk**. Some horses also trotted, cantered or galloped facing at an angle, or even side-on to their direction of forward movement, on the way to the barrier. We recorded this behaviour as **Tracking**.

And finally, from the newspaper racing results the next day, we copied each horse's **Handicap weight**, **Starting price**, and **Finishing position** into the data sheets.

We set up a modest bank for betting on behaviour. But being smart punters we waited until our fitness had improved slightly, so that we could keep up with all the horses, and until we thought we could pick out a winner. We had our first bet on 12 March 1990, at the Australian Cup meeting at Flemington. We backed The Phantom, who had not an ounce of spare fat, the most beautifully defined biceps and semitendinosus muscles you have ever seen, and a coat so glossy we could see our reflections. He finished down the track behind the bold, daggy front runner, Vo Rogue. And we soon relearnt Malcolm's life lesson. If we had to run to keep up with the horses going from the parade ring up to the mounting yard, we now had to sprint to a tote window to get a bet on before they jumped. Our fitness approached the level of elite athletes.

In all we had some 24 bets, three or four per meeting. And, I regret to report, we had only two collects. Our disappointment with The Phantom slowly turned to discouragement, and eventually to downright disillusionment. Our good-looking horses got hammered. Sweaty horses were winning races. Horses with magnificent glossy coats ran like also-rans. We stopped betting altogether. The spring left our step. We were left wondering - why were we chasing racehorses? We decided to terminate the study at 10 race meetings, and dragged ourselves along to the last few meetings, and even then we didn't finish it till May 1991. We consoled ourselves. It was only a little looksee, after all. A pilot study, and we were just flying by the seat of our pants. Marie went back to her studies, handed in her thesis and took herself off to Edinburgh to work on the cognitive behaviour of chickens. Can chooks really think? What a comedown from the sport of kings! I filed the data sheets away where scientists normally file failed experiments, at the very back of the bottom drawer of my filing cabinet. They were in a file called Punter's Revenge. Huh! Some revenge. There they gathered dust.

Chapter 3 Eureka!

I'm a mildly obsessive and compulsive person, as has already been noted. Something nagged away at me, and it wasn't The Missus, for wasting all that time on the horses. It was guilt. I've always written up and published every other research project I've worked on. Why should this be different? Simply because I was not being funded by the government? Because we had lost our own meagre research funds? Even failed experiments should be reported, if only to save others from the trouble of repeating our mistakes.

I decided to stiffen my resolve. I would go into the university computer room at night, whenever I had a chance, and enter the data into the VAX computer.

And so I did. Each race meeting took me several nights of work, line by line, converting "Rangy type", "Poor coat", and "Medium fitness" into numbers. Fortunately, the university threw out a whole heap of old VT100 terminals, computer dinosaurs, and I managed to scab one. I took it home, and with a 1400-baud modem, can you believe it, I could dial up the VAX. My enthusiasm slowly returned. It became my secret project. Buried in the basement, looking at the green phosphor screen, talking to the VAX, dreaming again. Not of untold wealth, but of salvaging something from the wreckage. I would write it up, regardless.

When all the data were finally entered into the VAX computer it was with great pleasure and anticipation that I typed in the command line:

```
$ SPSSX/OUTPUT=EXPLORE.OUT REVENGE.COM
```

and hit the return key. This was a command to the computer to run an exploratory analysis of the data using the well-known statistical program, SPSS (Statistical Package for the Social Sciences). The results of the analysis were simple descriptive statistics, such as means, medians, standard deviations and ranges.

You would have to say that the first results were very average. Indeed, the average racehorse was a *Light/Good* type, in *Good* condition and of *Good* fitness, had a *Normal* to *Glossy* coat, was not sweating, on a 17 cm strap, under *Firm* strapper hold, with a *Normal* head posture, with ears between *Forwards* and *Sideways*, tail between *Relaxed* and *Stiff*, and not aroused. On the track with the jockey up this horse held its head between *Down* and *Normal*, its neck was *Normal* and mouth *Open*. Few horses wore bandages, had a fast gait, tracked sideways or were led. Forty percent wore blinkers.

The next question for the computer was the big one. Did any of the 19 variables affect a horse's finishing position? However, before answering this question, the computer told me that I had a minor problem. The number of horses per race varied from a minimum of five to a maximum of 19, with an average of 13 horses. How did I expect it to compare a horse that finished second in a five horse race, with a horse that finished fifth in a field of 14? I decided that I needed to use another variable, which I called **Place**. To calculate **Place** I divided the finishing order into five 20-percent intervals, called percentiles, (1-20%, 21-40%, 41-60%, 61-80%, 81-100%). So, a horse finishing second in a five horse race would be in the second place percentile (2/5 = 40%), a horse finishing third out of 19 would be in the first place percentile (3/19 = 15.8%). At last, I could ask the computer the crunch question - did any of the 19 variables influence a horse's **Place**?

The results were very disappointing. Of the 19 horse appearance and behaviour variables only three, **Tail position**, **Neck angle - jockey up**, and **Resisting the bit** showed a significant relationship with **Place**. In addition, the power of these variables to indicate winning horses was extremely poor, especially when compared with a traditional variable such as **Starting price**. This is best illustrated in Figure 3.1.

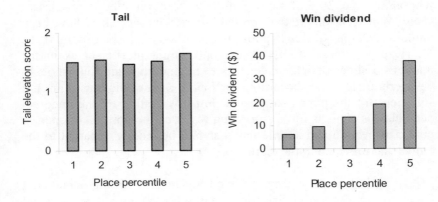

Figure 3.1
Comparison of tail elevation and totalisator win dividend according to finishing position.
Reprinted from Applied Animal Behaviour Science 53,G.D. Hutson and M.J. Haskell, Pre-race behaviour of horses as a predictor of race finishing order, 231-248, 1997, with permission from Elsevier Science.

There was a dramatic difference in starting price (the totalisator win dividend) between horses finishing in all of the five **Place** percentiles. In contrast, there were barely perceptible differences in tail elevation score. The implication was quite clear. You could do much better at the races by looking at the totalisator odds than by looking at the tails of horses.

I was disappointed, but not disconsolate. After all, we had found this out for ourselves when betting on the track. Also, I knew that many horse racing experts argue that the market price is the most reliable indicator of a horse's performance and that all information that will affect the price of a horse is known to all participants in the market and is quickly reflected in the market. This is known as the efficient market hypothesis. As an example, horses starting at a price of 4/1 (or with a winning chance of 1/5 or 20%), should in an efficient market, win on average, 20% of races. Similarly, horses in other odds classes should win according to their probability of winning. There have been numerous studies of this hypothesis using horse race betting markets. Nearly all of these studies detect only slight inefficiencies in the market - a slight bias for favourites to be underbet and long shots to be overbet. However, according to Wayne Snyder the biases are not sufficient for the punter to make a profit by betting on the underbet odds classes. This is not a surprising result as the horses are open to public inspection and simple faults should be readily apparent to the crowd and reflected in the market price.

But I didn't give up and re-stiffened my resolve. Being a punter, I knew that a more useful classification of a horse may not be its actual **Place** percentile, or where it finishes in the field, but whether it finishes up the front. Is it likely to be a winner, or maybe grab second or third place? So, the next step in my analysis was to compare the appearance and behaviour of likely winners with that of horses finishing down the track. In other words, I would compare horses finishing in the first 20-percentile with the rest, i.e. those in the last 80-percentile. And if I was going to compare winners with the rest I may as well compare losers with the rest, i.e. horses finishing in the last 20-percentile with those in the first 80-percentile.

The results were quite interesting. Both winners and losers could be significantly distinguished from other horses on the basis of their **Handicap weight** and **Starting price**. Winners carried more weight and started at shorter prices than other horses. Losers carried less weight and started at longer prices than other horses. Winners also had significantly better **Fitness** and had lower **Head positions**. Losers could be distinguished from other horses on the basis of a more elevated **Tail position** and a higher **Neck angle** with the jockey up. There was also a slight tendency for losers to be held in a firm **Strapper hold** and **Led by the clerk** of the course.

So, to summarise this exploratory analysis, although few behavioural variables were significant predictors of winning or losing performance, winners tended to be fitter and more relaxed, and losers tended to be more aroused, and required greater control. However, the predictive power of these single variables was still poor when compared with the traditional variables of **Handicap weight** and **Starting price**.

One problem with analysis of each of the 19 appearance and behaviour variables separately is that relationships or associations between variables may be overlooked. In an attempt to overcome this problem I decided it was time to call in the statistical big guns - multivariate discriminant analysis. Although this sounds scary and complicated, it is in fact quite easy to understand. But if you do get frightened, just skip ahead a few paragraphs to the bathroom scene.

Discriminant analysis is simply a statistical technique used to distinguish between two groups by using not single variables, as I did when exploring the data, but combinations of variables. The two groups I wanted to discriminate between were winners and losers. So I did two analyses, the first to distinguish winners (the first 20-percentile) from other horses and the second to distinguish losers (the last 20-percentile) from other horses. The output from the analysis is a magic formula, with loadings for each of the key variables. Unimportant variables are tossed out by the computer. And because I had two separate groups of data, with half the horses racing at Moonee Valley and half at Flemington, I used only the Moonee Valley data to work out my formulae. Then I would be able to see if they were any good at predicting winners or losers by testing them on the Flemington results.

Six variables were required in the formula for picking losers. They were **Starting price**, **Neck angle - jockey up**, **Strapper hold**, **Handicap weight**, **Led by clerk** and **Bandages**. In contrast, 11 variables were required in the formula for picking winners.

The next step was to use these formulae to predict losers at Flemington. Of the 458 horses that we observed at Flemington, 104 finished in the last 20-percentile. The magic formula predicted that 46 horses would finish in the last percentile. 31 of these predictions were right and 15 wrong, a strike rate of 31/46, or 67.4%. Two thirds of the losing predictions were correct! In contrast, the magic formula for winners predicted that 32 horses would finish in the first 20-percentile. Only nine of these predictions were correct, an accuracy of 9/32, or 28.1%.

So, in summary, horses finishing at the tail of the field could be predicted using six variables and with an accuracy of nearly 70%, whereas nearly double the number of variables were needed to predict winners, but with less than half the accuracy. Another more subtle conclusion could also be made. Variables, which were seemingly unimportant, based on their lack of significance in the single variable tests, could supply important information and be extremely useful in the multivariate model. This implies that behaviour and appearance variables deemed unimportant on their own to the casual observer may in fact provide potentially rewarding information.

Scientists love the story of Archimedes jumping out of his bath and running naked down the street shouting "Eureka!" I can't say that I had such a sudden inspiration. Rather, I very slowly floated to the top of my bath and realised that I had cracked it. I might be an ordinary scientist with a drinking and gambling problem, and decidedly dicey health, but I can recognise a Nobel prize underwater. I didn't stop smiling for two weeks. Science and some fancy statistics had turned around what we thought was a dismal failure into a major discovery. As well, it had turned around our whole way of thinking about racehorses. We could pick losers! We had set out on this study hoping to detect single behaviour or appearance variables, which would allow us to predict race winners. However, we found that none of these single variables could improve upon the predictions made using the betting market. But when more than one variable was considered, behaviour and appearance variables were valuable in eliminating horses that could not win. As Marie and I were to later write in our paper:

This information has potentially high economic worth.

Our paper on "Pre-race behaviour of horses as a predictor of race finishing order" was submitted to the editor of *Applied Animal Behaviour Science* on February 2, 1996. Nearly seven long years had passed since that optimistic journey down Racecourse Road. That is a lot of nights, and a lot of stiff resolve. The paper was finally published in early March 1997.

Chapter 4 Fifteen minutes of fame

Thursday 31 October 1996

It must be around 11.00 am and the phone rings. Ian O'Neill, producer of the Clive Robertson show on 2GB. Just heard about the story in *New Scientist*. I inwardly sigh. Oh, no. *New Scientist* is not meant to come out in London until Saturday, and I never get it till Monday here. I had only anticipated one day of madness. This is Thursday. Can I do an interview on Monday at 6.55 am? 6.55 am? I groan. Never been much of a one for the early morning gallops. Phone rings again. The Ron Casey show. Just seen the wire service on my horse stuff. What station are you? 2GB! They drop it once they find out they've been scooped by Clive. *The Age* rings and I ask them to fax me a copy of the wire. At last I get to see what the sudden fuss is about. *New Scientist* has obviously released the story early to cash in on Cup fever.

Here's the wire:

> **London, October 31.** Punters were given a valuable racing tip by an animal behaviour expert today - how to pick a likely winner by spotting the losers before the race. According to Australian expert Geoff Hutson horses without a hope give themselves away in the mounting yard and during the approach to the starting gate. Hutson, from Melbourne University, and PhD student Marie Haskell spent 20 months studying the appearance and behaviour of 867 horses entered in 67 races. Each horse was given a score based on 29 variables, 19 of which were linked with behaviour and appearance. The rest were based on information from the race book like the jockey, the horse's age and sex, and the odds at the tote. Hutson told *New Scientist* magazine: "We reckon we have six variables that will help the punter recognise a loser. In other words, you can narrow down the field, thereby increasing your chances of picking a winner. If you could eliminate enough horses, you could bet on the field and come out on top."

Two of the variables are unsurprising - starting odds and how much weight the horse is carrying. Long shots given a low weight by handicappers had little chance of winning. But Hutson and Haskell found that when four other variables were added to the equation the chances of spotting losers was even higher. These were the angle of the head (it should be at about 45°); how tightly the horse has to be held when being led round the mounting yard (it should be loosely); whether the horse requires handling by the clerk of the course before entering the starting gate (it should not); and whether the horse has any bandages which may conceal an injury.

Hutson said: "If you spotted a horse with a combination of these variables, then I'd go straight to the bar rather than the bookie." During the study 67.4 per cent of his losing predictions were correct. He added "In general, the more relaxed the racehorse, the more chance it had of winning." As for the Melbourne Cup, Hutson's tip is Irish St Leger winner Oscar Schindler. "Its condition looked perfect on television," he said. "But if it acted up in the mounting yard then I might change my mind."

Ah, Cup fever. I love it. But I sense I'm in for a tough carnival this year. It's Thursday, for Chrissakes. Thank goodness I'm taking a week of annual leave for the Big One.

About 12 midday. Do my first interview, Jo Jarvis, ABC World Today. I mark myself at six out of 10. Just warming up. I plan some answers and start remembering my old advice to myself from previous times when I've been famous: to take control of the direction of the interview from the first question. If it's the wrong question, turn it around to ask yourself the right one. Learn from the politicians. Next up Jane Murphy, Radio Australia. I'm in form. 9/10.

The mobile phone rings in my bag. My mobile phone never rings in my bag, mainly because it's never turned on. The only previous time was when I had accidentally left it on, and even then it was a wrong number. It's solely for emergency breakdowns in the 1955 FJ Holden Special Sedan, my now rusting Australian icon. Some enterprising journos have looked me up in the phonebook and have called home. They got the number through my daughter. It's sheer accident that it's on.

More interviews. Derryn Hinch wants me. Shame! But I'm already doing 2GB. More calls. I make a heap of bookings for Friday. The Agriculture Faculty Marketing Manager rings me. Wants to know what the fuss is about and why don't they know about it. Hmmph! What's the university ever done for me? They want to cash in on me being famous. I send her the Abstract of my now famous paper. The university Media Manager rings me. Tells me that it'll get worse before it gets better, do I need any help, a lot of scientists don't know what to say in an interview. I tell her it's cool. I'm from the school that believes any publicity is good publicity, as long as they spell your name right. She relaxes, and tells me to enjoy it. And I confirm that's exactly what I'm about to do. People never remember what you say, they just remember that they heard you. This is my 15 minutes of fame, and I'm going to enjoy, enjoy. I'm an existentialist, and this is my life.

I get home to find The Missus has picked up my Mum. It's her birthday - 83! She likes it when I'm famous. And she reminds me of her philosophy - all publicity is good publicity, son, just make sure they spell your name right!

Back from taking her home and I've just missed BBC London calling. The phone rings again. It's Jeremy from the *Daily Mirror*. Wants to talk about the horses. I can see the headline now: Scientist Picks Losers! No doubt the story will be sandwiched in between some breasts! The phone rings again. BBC London. We book a time for tomorrow. It's 11 blooming 30. Phone rings again. Jeremy. Excuse me Dr Hutson, how old are you. I can't stop laughing. I yell out to The Missus, the *Daily Mirror* wants to know how old I am - should I tell 'em? She wants me to say 50, but I can't lie - I am 49! The kids, sorry, young adults, want a piece of the action. They too want to be in the *Daily Mirror*. I tell Jeremy I have two children,

Ruth, 20, and Kate, 17. What do they think about you betting? I tell Jeremy that they both roll their eyes. I can see the headline now - Melbourne Dad (49) Picks Losers Scientifically. Children Ruth (20) and Kate (17) roll their eyes. Ah, my first day of fame.

Friday 1 November

Up at 6.30 am. The day my father died. The spring carnival has never been the same since. Can't even think about it before the phone rings. 3AW, another program, not the Neil Mitchell show, trying to track down Marie Haskell. They too want to run with the story. Marie's in Edinburgh studying thought processes in chooks. Phone rings again, Mitchell program, checking the time for my interview. First interview is at 7.45. Peter Thompson, Radio National. A quickie, only three or four minutes, which is not enough time. I give my condensed version. Good, though. The billy lids and The Missus enjoy eavesdropping. 8/10. Then off to work. Another interview is lined up for 8.35. I'd better speed up. The icon hits 85 kmh. The mobile rings in my car! My mobile has never rung in my car! It's 3AW, wanting to do me early, while it's hot! 8.35. 6WF, Perth. Michael Schultz. 8/10. 9.00. Neil Mitchell, 3AW. I have to listen to endless advertisements before finally getting to air. He gives me plenty of time, and takes call back after I'm off the air. An average 7/10. Too commercial. The doctor bit gave him the irrits. Just a bit of Cup fever. 10.30. Jeremy Cordeaux, 5DN Adelaide. I stop marking myself now. 12.00. Annie Hastwell, ABC Darwin. Then more calls. TV3 New Zealand wants to do a live cross. Can I get to Channel 7 by 4.30? I tell them I've got the BBC at 3.30. Phone rings at 2.50. Am I in the car on the way? I reply that the BBC is not coming through till 3.30. The producer realises she's too anxious, and is one hour ahead of herself.

The media manager rings to see how I'm coping. Cool, cool. I'm enjoying it. Getting a little bit hyper, little bit tired. 3.30. Rod Sharp, BBC. Sports show of some sort. They replay the call of the 95 Cup. Very atmospheric. As soon as I'm on you can detect that they don't like convict colonials. I've come across this before. It gets right up the Brits' nostrils if someone from Down Under is an expert on any topic, especially if it's one they fancy themselves. They read from an article about me on page four of *The Times*, and then quote a bookie, I think William Hill, bagging me. They have an expert on line to tackle me about track going, but that's easy. We only scored them on good or better. I tip them Oscar on looks. I've tipped him everywhere on looks. But my bottom line, as always, is to check him in the yard.

Off over Westgate in the icon. My mobile rings. It's Marco Bass, Today Tonight producer, confirming our date at the horse wash after Race 2 on Derby Day. Channel 7. Kevin takes me through a veritable rabbit warren. I've never done a studio interview before, always outside. I let myself be a little bit nervous. To make-up. Lots of polyfilla into the cracks around the eyes. To the studio. I'm looking at the camera, but no picture feedback. Someone's talking to me in my ear, but I can't see them. I ask for a shot of what I look like. They swivel the monitor and I'm sitting at a desk with a backdrop of Melbourne. I reckon I look a bit stiff, wooden, cardboard cutout scientist. G'day, Bill. G'day New Zealand! .... I start marking myself again, 5/10. But good experience. I need more practice looking into the ether and being interviewed by an invisible interviewer in my ear. To make-up, to get it off. Jill Singer is discussing what dress she will wear to the Derby with the make-up girls. I like the white one with black spots.

Home. And then I pick up Jenny Chandler at the Marco Polo Motel. She works at the Animal Behaviour Research Centre in New Zealand and I met her on a visit there a year or two ago. She's over here with that noted mud runner Van Der Hum, the 1976 Cup winner – number 6, five-year-old chestnut gelding, R.J. Skelton, cerise, green diagonal stripes, armbands and cap, barrier 23, SP 9/2. She's lost and lonely in Melbourne, so I've promised her a trip highlight of pizza at the Kensington Pizza Parlour. The No. 1 is most excellent. We join Steve Alomes and Cate Jones there. I've asked Steve because he's a rival academic who likes getting his mug on TV and in the papers, so it's a good night to boast and compare notes. Jenny started riding The Hum when he retired. She retells the story that all Aussies hate to hear about a previous Cup winner. His last race was a jumps race and he fell. But it was a clean fall and the jockey remounted to finish and take third place! She's now taken over the ownership of the horse. She reckons I should ride him. Me? Don't be a "wuss", she reckons. A "wuss"?

We ask if the VRC is looking after her nicely. She reports that she's had to pay her own way. Fosters are sponsoring half the horse, and the VRC the other half. I think it's miserable. I offer to write a letter to Brian Beattie, the CEO of the VRC.

At last to bed. Still haven't thought about my Dad. Must be the first anniversary ever I haven't thought about it. I reckon he would have been proud.

Saturday 2 November. Derby Day

Today I rode a Cup winner. Can you believe it! Normally, I never mount or ride anything that's more than two feet off the ground, so that only leaves motorbikes. I certainly wouldn't put my leg over something that moved if it was animal. But today, here I am, 8.15 am on the morning of the greatest day's racing on earth, sitting on Van Der Hum. And I've got a photo to prove it (Photo 3). I'm no "wuss".

Time to set off for the track, walking from my place. It's hot. Too hot. I put on my sunscreen, check my trouser pocket, binoculars, class ratings, and select my Crown Casino cap. We're off. As soon as we hit the turnstiles my mobile rings. It's Marco, producer of Today Tonight, checking where I am. I say I'll be there in two minutes. Boy, I betcha Jenny's impressed! I meet Peter Hutchinson, the smiling jockey, and the TV crew at the horse wash. The boys are gossiping waggishly about their previous interviewee, Lloyd Williams. He gets so nervous during interviews that they accuse the

Photo 3
Van Der Hum and Geoffrey.

assistant producer of having him in a squirrel grip. When she denies this, they suggest that she must have some good compromising photos. I wonder what they'll say about me? We do the interview leaning over the parade ring rail. Peter stumbles on a couple of lines and we have to do a couple of retakes. Marco directs us to chat while they shoot from behind. Peter is a lovely feller. And I suppose that's why he's struggling to get rides. He's too nice, people don't take him seriously. I remember he had a bad fall, too. Was it Caulfield? That's half the interview in the can, and we agree to meet before the Mackinnon to film me checking out the weight-for-age stars. We check a few horses in the birdcage. Gold Ace looks nice. Lion Hunter has a green bag over his head. That sure is some pacifier!

We'll have time to watch the main race. To the finish line. I leave Jenny at the GG-spot, a small bump on the lawn that provides excellent views of the finish, and have a small bet on Ebony Grosve, sight unseen. It's the main race on the main day. I've gotta have at least one bet. Ebony Grosve's tailed off last, but runs home nicely.

Quite happy to give a young horse time to settle in its first try at a distance. Looks like a nice horse. Back to the parade ring. Marco says the camera crew has been pulled off to do another story. Probably a hat story, I'd say. He reckons they've got enough in the can to do the story. I ask Marco if he can get me a free ticket to The Cup. Just trying it on. The media use you up and you get nothing in return. He says complimentary tickets are as rare as hen's teeth, but he'll see what he can do. I'm not going to hold my breath.

We check the Mackinnon horses anyway. We rule out six, but I can't tell you why because we were just yelling it out to the imaginary camera and I didn't make notes in my race book. I don't like Nothin' Leica Dane because he's been doing laps since we arrived at the track. He must be up to 20,000 now. Ruled out Octagonal, Magnet Bay, Skybeau, Love Dance, and Circles of Gold. I remember two thirds of the field, the best in the land, had tapes of some sort.

I back Gold Ace in the next. Lion Hunter looks fat, and they hold him back to the last minute. The clerk grabs Gold Ace, but I explain to Jenny that you never get fussed about that if it is saddlecloth number 1 or the favourite. It's very reassuring when Gold Ace bolts in.

If my account of the greatest day's racing on earth seems disjointed, maybe rudimentary, perhaps sketchy at best. There is an excuse. It was a very hot day and I was very thirsty. My memory is not what it was. I can barely remember arriving home very tired and emotional.

Sunday 3 November

An interview with Andre Kassay and Shane Templeton on Correct Weight. I tell the boys a bit about what I saw on Derby Day. The sprint, a three horse race between Encosta De Lago, Gold Ace and the boom sprinter Lion Hunter. We ruled out Encosta because of the wide barrier draw. Seems crazy, doesn't it, in barrier one, but they've over-watered the inside of the track. That leaves Gold Ace, the class horse, and Lion Hunter. Didja see Lion Hunter in the birdcage? He had a green bag on his head. Horses with green bags on their head don't win many races. So we backed Gold Ace. The boys seemed quite impressed. I tell them about the Mackinnon. The Dane had already done 20,000 laps of the ring before the race, so we ruled him out. And as Octagonal walked passed there was a window of opportunity when we got to see straight into his brain. We saw a serious mental problem. The boys liked that!

Sunday night

The *Hong Kong Times* rings and arranges an interview for tomorrow. I tell them that I can probably fit them in at 10.30 am. The phone rings again! It's the brother-in-law, William Mole. I hear you just had a call from Hong Kong. Oh, no. He got me a real beauty!!

Monday 4 November

Up at 6.30 am. Phone rings. Clive Robertson show just checking if I'm conscious. Again at 6.55. I'm deferred till after the news. That's good, less time pressure. They ring again and I'm on. Sardonic bastard. Doesn't give two hoots for Cup fever. So I play it up a bit. He likes my line about losing all our research funds. In the end, he doesn't even want my Cup tip. That's style!

Then to work. 10.15 am. 5MV, Jim Griffas, South Australia. 11.00. 2BL, Richard Glover. Triple J ring. We roll the tape and do one on the spot. They're a rock music station, aren't they? Then The Cup sweep. Oh, no, I've agreed to organise the sweep since the secretary has taken the package. I draw all the horses then realise I've left myself out! Probably not a bad thing because they're all still dirty on me for taking the quinella in the Caulfield Cup sweep.

The phone refuses to stop ringing. Punters. Every punter in Australia seems to be ringing me up. The university ring. They want to photograph me for their glossy publications. Meet the photographer at Phar Lap at 4.00 pm. Off again. I try to go in the back door of the Melbourne Museum, where Phar Lap used to be when I was a lad. It's locked. To the front door. The most wonderful revolving door in the whole world is gone! We used to love coming here just to go through that door! Round and round. Sliding glass has a lot to answer for. And you pay! Five bucks! But there's Phar Lap. Still the same. Michael Silver shoots off three rolls of film! Gosh, what if I had split the atom or something!

And then I have time to fully take in where I am. This is a holy shrine. The holiest of holy shrines. A shrine to the spirit of racing. And I'm here, on Cup Eve! I sit down and pay my respects. The 10-minute video. The relics. The currycomb, the bridle and bits, the speculation about colic or arsenic. You know, you can be moved by this stuff. And how his body bits are spread out all out over the world. The bones in Wellington, New Zealand, the heart in Canberra, the skin before my eyes. Photographs of how he was made, the bits of string under his skin to reproduce his veins. He was a big horse, fabulous colour. A blaring loudspeaker interrupts my contemplation and tells me to go home. The souvenir shop is closing. I manage to duck in a buy a Phar Lap pin.

As I stride from the museum I put the pin in my lapel. I am empowered by the spirit of Phar Lap. The tingles rage up and down my spine. I can feel the adrenalin surging through every part of my body, along the bits of string under my skin. I am empowered. I am alive. I am very much alive. I feel like Major Les Hiddins, reaching the top of that mountain. It doesn't get any better than this....

We watch Today Tonight. Hutchy's interviewing all the experts. Bart Cummings, Gai Waterhouse, Dr Turf, Subzero. Hey, that's me, on TV! And they splice in some nice shots of horses doing bad behaviour. Good! A neighbour, Annie Cantwell rings up. Just saw me on TV. Do I want to borrow her spare Members' ticket for Cup Day? I knew Marco would come good.

Tuesday 5 November. Cup Day

Up early, 6.30 am, to go to work. My animal technician has taken the long weekend off and the student I hire for back-up has gone to Sydney. I've got to go out to The Farm and feed the blooming beasts myself. Weigh day, too. It'll take twice as long. I finish by 10.30, a quick check of the email. Everyone wants to know why I'm famous. I flash back that I have no time to reply, I'm off to The Cup. I have media commitments! I suggest that by 3.30 this arvo the only people interested in reading my story will be in the fish and chip shop.

Home in time to hear the choppers roaring over my place. Kensington is like the Vietnam War on Cup Day. Off to the TAB with all the bets for the mother, mother-in-law, father-in-law, The Missus, and billy lids. Each year I vow and declare that I won't put them on and run the book myself. But they like holding real tickets that they can tear up later. The tote's been down and everyone's frustrated. Long queues. As if by some miracle my line suddenly rockets forward and we get on. Oh, no, is that an omen? Divine intervention?

And I'm off, to The Cup. Phar Lap pin in lapel, binoculars, lunch. Kiss, kiss, kiss. I get out into the street and realise I've forgotten my bankroll. You'd think I'd never been to the races before. I'm off, again. The Irish neighbours down the road spot me and yell out good luck, Oscar. I pass John Duggan's place and he says he saw me on TV last night. I tell him I'm going for the Irish horse. A van screeches to a stop. It's Craig, the local newsagent, delivering Best Bets to his paper boy on the corner near the course. He gives me a lift. I tell him I'm famous, and he looks me straight in the eye and says "Were you that Doctor? I thought it was Doctor Turf!" We discuss trifectas. He usually boxes 4 and 7 with the two favourites. Was $1800 ahead after the first two races on Derby Day, finished with $160. The paperboy has buggered off, and Craig has a mountain of Best Bets. He gives me one. I see they tip Saintly. I walk into the course, and being an old lag, wait for the free bus to the gate. We drive through the car park and I get my first glimpse of the drunks. Gosh, and it's only midday. The bus is waved to a halt and boarded by two lady drunks, an angel and a pregnant nun. They are absolutely pissed. They bless all the passengers on the bus. I meekly ask for God's tip. But I already know the omen bet. Saintly.

I stride through the gate into the course. My tips? I've left my blooming class ratings at home. My hat? Where's my blooming hat? My sunscreen, I forgot the blooming sunscreen. What did I remember, I wonder. I go to Information to find out where I can buy a Melbourne Cup hat. They direct me to a stall all of five metres away which I probably walked past trying to find out where it was. I select a pale blue cap. I ask the drunk next to me what it looks like and she says she prefers the other one, the brown one. I see I'm in for a tough day. I stick with my own choice. A quick scan of the crowd. Five Elvises, two fake Scotsmen (they can't be for real as they ain't got no dirks in their socks), three sultans, three belly dancers, one Jesus Will Save You (oh, no), a heap of Mad Hatters, and not a gorilla or Superman in sight. They're dressing down this year.

I check out the horse stalls. Hum's in 104. Oscar's in 126. I know exactly where that is. VIP area, behind the hedge, away from the rubberneckers. I head to the parade ring to meet the SBS crew. Now, no sniggering. It's cool to be a multi-cultural multi-media super star. We agree to meet in 10 minutes to give me time to make my bet. I notice The Dane doing his walking exercise in the ring. The couple in front of me are making proud noises. I check my race book, and realise that since I wasn't standing behind T.J. Smith, this must be Mr Hodge and Mrs Dalton. I point to their names in the book and seek confirmation of their ID. They confirm and tip me The Dane. I ask Mr Hodge if The Dane is getting a bit stalliony, but he says he's OK. So I line up to bet. And what was my bet, I hear you ask? $1000 on the nose of Oscar? I take a 6x7x8 multiple trifecta on The Cup. $108 for 50 cents. And just as I'm about to leave the window, I suppose I've gotta have a $100 on Oscar's nose. I mean, I'm locked

in, I've tipped him to the whole world, and I've never even seen him!
I'd better put my money where my mouth is.

Then we do the interview, leaning on the fence in the birdcage. I can
nearly do it standing on my head now. These are very useful multi-
cultural multi-media skills I'm picking up. Then a foray into the
betting ring. There's no mike, just a colour shot, so I have great fun
walking up to the bookie saying that you think I'm going to give you
this $50 don't you, but the cameraman just wants to film me punting
on Oscar, and I'd prefer you gave me some of your money instead.
Then I have half an hour before we suss out The Cup horses in the
ring. I remember my neighbour Neal Bethune's invite to check out
the Channel 10 studio, so I knock him up. They're doing an
interview, so I have to wait. At last I'm in and they're cleaning the
make-up off Tom Keneally. Been there, done that. He's in top hat
and tails with a very impressive VIP super-important guest badge on
his lapel. I'm tempted to draw his attention to my Phar Lap badge,
but I settle instead for asking him if he's backed Oscar. He doesn't
reply. I guess he doesn't know that I'm famous and worth replying
to. The 10 set up is amazing. Neal, a freelance cameraman, lets me
listen to the director calling the shots on the 30-odd cameras around
the course. I hear him complaining about how Roy the Boy looks -
too red and sweaty. The blimp shot is brilliant. I meet Tim Webster
and ask about tips. Their tip is that the floor manager won't get their
Cup bets on.

Time to look at the horses with the crew over my shoulder. There's
Jenny and The Hum. Doesn't he look great for 25 years old. Coat's a
bit dry, muzzle's not too grey though, backbone is very bony, loin a
bit hollow, but great. I boast to all in the near vicinity that I've ridden
a Cup winner. They think I'm just another Cup crazy. There's the
Governor-General, Sir William Dean. I'd pass him in the street and
wouldn't recognise him. But then I'm a republican. There's The
Dane, looks good, relaxed. Beaux Art. Bandaged on all four. Yucko!
There's Oscar. First impression. Oh no, a nose roll. Oh no, I hate
nose rolls. I know, I know, Kingston Rule had a nose roll. Second

impression, breathtaking. Absolutely breathtaking. Big, red, imposing. The reincarnation of Phar Lap. Third impression. A strapper's horse, all plaited mane and chequerboard rump. Show pony, but no pony. And, oh no, he's swishing his tail! And, is that head up!! No, his head's OK again now. Help. Panic. Fourth impression. Why does he have three strappers? I turn to the camera. "I like the favourite". Turn away, bite my tongue, cross my fingers. Oh no, I've backed him and tipped him to the world and he's swishing his tail and has got his head up. Tail swishers can still win races, but not if there's something else wrong with them. Did I really see his head up? It's very worrying. The crew starts hassling me to slag some horses. Beaux Art, number one slag, surefire loser, then My Kiwi Gold, rotten head, tail too stiff, Sapio, no way, Centico, hopeless, are all duly slagged. Alcove, bandaged, looks too light. I see a problem with Circles of Gold. But when I get home I find the middle pages have fallen out of my race book! Who knows what it was. They're trying to interview me and I can't even see the horses. Where's Doriemus, Saintly?? It's bedlam. There's the NZedder, Senator. Looks great, hard, fit, a real stayer. He's just a bit distracted by the crowd. Looking over the fence. They've gone! They've gone up to the mounting yard.

We watch the race from the 400. You can't hear the course broadcast from here. No one has a radio, and I'm the only one with binos. They're off! As they go past us I call Oscar's position. There's six behind him. I yell out "Sixteenth". I don't see them again until they're round the back, and I call the first six, Grey Shot, Few Are Chosen, what's he doing up there, The Dane, he's close, Super Slew, Court of Honour, Saintly, looks great on the rails, can't see Oscar. They sweep into the straight past us, The Dane just in front, but Saintly is in second gear and I know straight away he's got it won. I bet Bart had it relaxed in the yard. The camera crew pack up and go home. They don't even want to film the famous scientist tearing up his tickets.

I wander up towards the mounting yard, against the stream of human traffic, going home. I'm a bit down. I see Count Chivas grabbed second, Skybeau third. That blooming Count Chivas, my number one selection last year, has cost me thousands in the trifecta this year. They replay the race on the Big Screen and I get to see it properly for the first time. I remark to the bloke next to me that Count Chivas still gets second. We commiserate with each other. He had boxed Saintly and Skybeau too, but not The Count. The bloke next to him says, g'day Geoff. It's Brian Leury from work. He didn't see the race because he was stuck out the back. Brian reckons he'd rather see Essendon win a Grand Final than go to the Melbourne Cup. Now, I like the races, but I reckon he's dead-set right about that!

I get a beer and sit down to take in the post-Cup atmosphere. At last, I can relax. Look, there's a lady, drunk. But she's a much older person, unconscious, spew down the front of her beautiful blue satin frock. Head slumped, lacy white hat awry. What can I count here:

- two bananas in pyjamas
- one only viking
- five pirates with shoulder parrots
- 15 Shoalhaven rugby players
- one punter, complete in check sports jacket, fair dinkum pork pie steward's hat, horn-rimmed glasses, one of those old National 10 transistor radios in a leather case, binoculars, and form guide. A genuine relic
- three Santas
- one pair of very long legs, under a very short skirt, say 150 mm short, and a very large fluffy purple hat, say 1250 mm long!
- 2000 jester and joker hats - someone's got a nice concession
- two policepersons posing for photos with drunks. Now, there's tolerance
- two drag queens
- two Boy Scouts, who collect my can.

Most popular material - a luminous, technicolour print with black footprints all over it. I've seen five ladies and gents outfits made from it. Must be on special at Spotlight. The Queen goes past. Her Royal Highness, the Queen Elizabeth, in rubber mask and flowing crimson red cape. She turns to face the crowd and throws open the cape, to reveal an enormous set of naked rubber tits. It's stunning. We're all very shocked. A champagne cork pops and lands in my lap. My first for the day.

I go into the Members for the last. Top deck. Cold wind. Jim Marconi's Delsole, an old stager, looms up on the turn. He's running third!! Go, go, DELSOLE!! As soon as he hears me he collapses as if shot. Everyone high tails it. It's Cup Day, I'm on the top deck of the Members, looking out over the mounting yard. I am the only person in the whole stand. I survey the wonderful scene below. A sea of drunks, bathed in sunshine and noise.

I stroll past the rails bookies, Members' side. There's the largest hat in the world. I ask the escalator attendant if he reckons she's being paid to wear it. Have to be. It looks like a triffid with a clock on top. I saunter up to the wearer and ask her: Madam, are you being paid to wear that hat? She smiles and says, sort of. It's her clock company.

Out to the hoi polloi. One last beer. There's 20 of us lined up to get a beer, the sun is setting on the betting ring, and a girl walks past in a long, black lace, dress. The sun catches her silhouette and 20 drunks catch sight of a perfectly naked female form. She is wearing absolutely no underwear. There is an outbreak of whooping and hollering, and get it off, before the moment has passed.

A quick final reconnoiter of the Members' car park to see if I can scab a free drink from the brother-in-law's boot. No sign, but there's John Elliot, looking like the cat's pyjamas. I guess a car park is a heaps better place to be than the inside of a courtroom. I show the bronze Phar Lap statue my lapel badge. He thinks it's pretty spiffy. To the dunny. The drunk next to me asks what won The Cup.

Reckons he hasn't seen a race all day. I can believe that. Back to the train. They're all staggering now. I'm squeezed in and we sing "Swing low, sweet chariot", all the way back to North Melbourne.

Home in time to watch the SBS World News. Famous scientist backs Oscar. They cut out famous scientist slags Beaux Art, who finished last. The kids see the shot of Dad waving $50 at a bookie and pretend to be shocked. Time to give my Members' ticket back to Annie. She lost, too. Thanks, Annie, it was great. We run into my cousin, Barbara, and cousin-in-law, Chris Ward, on the street. Kensington is a very small suburb. They are Christians and of course Chris has backed the omen tip. As if I need reminding, Beadman's a born-again Christian, you know. I'll let him have the last word on The Cup .... "A bad day for existentialists!".

Wednesday 6 November

Wake up, 4.00 am. Nightmares. Oscar's swishing his tail in my face.

Up early, 6.30 am. Can't seem to sleep any more....

It's two o'clock, and the phone hasn't rung once. I guess life's back to normal. I can be an ordinary scientist again. Wait, ... it's ringing. Excuse me.... it's Tokyo calling, we want to do an interview. Is that you William? You've already got me once. That's not Hong Kong, is it? No, no, it's not a hoax, it's for real, Erikku from Tokyo. I tell him The Cup is over and I'm history. Yesterday's news. A very earnest voice tells me, oh no, we have a lot of Group One races here. I suddenly realise that the Japan Cup is huger than ours. I wonder if they want my tip.... I've got an excellent omen bet! Haven't seen him yet, though.

And another call from a professional punter in Perth. He's a fitness assessor, using "vascularity" - or in other words, evidence of visible veins. I tell him he should check out Phar Lap at the Melbourne

Museum. He's got outstanding veins and they've all been done with bits of string underneath the skin. He thinks that's a fabulous joke.

The mobile hasn't rung all day.

Thursday 7 November. Oaks Day

I'm off. Now, this time I remember the usual pocket-patting routine. Passport? Tickets? Money? I must be more relaxed. Sunscreened up, Melbourne Cup hat, binoculars, ratings, exchequer and lunch. Regular relic. I pass John Duggan's house. He's waiting to pounce. What happened to Oscar then? I describe what I saw and explain that I was locked in and I wasn't going to squib it after tipping him to the world. John, I was taken to the cleaners. Lost everything. Dead set broke. Tipped Beaux Art, though. Finished stone, motherless, last. Anyone can pick losers, Geoff.

It's a perfect Melbourne day. A gentle stroll. If Derby Day is Rollers, and The Cup is choppers, then today is yellow taxis, all moving at less than strolling pace. Thank goodness Chairman Jeff didn't have his way with pink. Another random thought. Thank goodness the Ming Dynasty didn't have his way with royals. Imagine having 100 royals on the nose of Oscar! I pass the man with the jester hat concession. How much? $15. Wish I had known that on Tuesday, my hat cost $20. But they don't keep much sun off.

It's crowded, seems to be more people than the Derby. I go to my normal lunch spot in the birdcage. Ah, I can just relax and eat, and enjoy my roast lamb and tomato sauce sandwich. A strapper goes past with a horse. In trouble. Poor head behaviour, I think. It soon escalates to the whole bit, rearing, bucking and lashing out behind. The strapper whisks it back towards its stall. Don't recognise the strapper. Damn! I've got to work. Jump up in a flash and follow that horse, down the back, round the side, what stall is that? You Remember! You bet I will! I get out my ratings and cross him out of Race 7. Back to lunch. But there's another horse being bad. Stop it. I want to rest. Fighting the strapper, tail, full bore. I follow it too. Well, I'll be buggered. I've just ruled a line through the favourite for the Oaks, Dashing Eagle!

The Oaks. I'd better have a bet. I check the horses in the parade ring and bad behaviour is rife. Heads are up, or twisted to one side. There are bandages, swishing tails, nose rolls, gait problems, sweating horses, forceful strappers, and pacifiers. So much bad behaviour! I cross out a heap of horses and decide to take a 4x4x7 multiple trifecta. But it looks like a lock-out coming up. Alan Stockdale, the Victorian Treasurer, is blocking the window. I wonder how much he will bet? $10,000? $50,000? I catch a flash of colour - purple. Five measly bucks? No wonder our economy is bouncing back. There are still lots of hats ahead of me in the queue. I consider the mobile, but I'm relaxed and get set with one minute to go. I watch the race on the Big Screen and the roughie gets up. Ah, well, that's racing. I loved putting the line through Dashing Eagle. Should've done the Dutch book. Should've boxed all seven horses in the trifecta. Should've, should've....

Back to my seat and the germ of an idea is taking hold. There is so much bad behaviour about that my 19 variables are clearly totally inadequate to describe it all. And why am I still betting on class ratings? If behaviour is so important, shouldn't I bet solely on that? Am I a pettifogger? Telling the world to bet on behaviour, and secretly clinging on to my class ratings? I squirm a bit on my seat. This is obviously a matter that will need serious attention when I'm a normal person again.

Up to the yard for the last race. Roy Higgins, the former jockey and now expert radio commentator, is doing his interview with Peter Donegan, standing on his box. It reminds me of Alan Ladd, except that they used to dig holes for his leading ladies to stand in. There's Marco and the boys, the Today Tonight crew! They're filming Hutchy returning to scale and explaining why his mount has just lost.

I wave but they don't see yesterday's hero. But I'm glad he got a ride, he's a very nice feller.

I make my way to the station. I only have to step over one unconscious dolly bird (sorry, young adult woman). I'd seen her before and all the boys were trying to look up her flapping skirt. Now someone's stuck her bag on her behind to hold it down. I remember that Tony, our work experience student, was coming to perv on the women. I don't have the energy to do the same, but just hope it's not one of my own daughters! The lawn is very squelchy, covered in shattered plastic cups. I know they've been watering the outside of the track, but surely not this far out? It must be beer and champagne. I definitely rate it Dead. Two refugees from Cup Day accost me. All top hat and tails and evening dress, with a Save Jesus placard. But it's not Jesus they want to save, but the ABC. They twist my arm till it hurts and I agree to write a letter to the Prime Minister about it.

The crowd surges onto the platform and I use Tuesday's ticket. I put my thumb over the date. I mean, I mean, I only want to go one stop.

Friday 8 November

Wake with the dawn chorus. Lie there till 6.30 am.

Today I have *Tokyo Today*. The phone rings at 9.15 am. Very professional, excellent English. I had faxed them the tricky words I use like punter, strapper, clerk of the course, but they are really cool. Their English is better than mine. They will ring precisely at 9.45 and as soon as I answer I'm on air. Do I have any questions? No. I can do this falling off a log. I imagine the famous disk jockey dialling me up on air .... Good morning, Jon. G'day Tokyo.... Then the phone rings.... Is that half an hour? I've made a mental note to cut down on the colloquialisms, but I can't help myself.... Good morning, Jon. G'day Tokyo.... Jon finishes the interview by asking what everyone asks - do I win? Well, I'm like most punters. I've had some big wins in my time and I've had some terrible losses, but the bottom line is this. I still have to report to the university each day for work. The day I retire is the day you'll know I'm rich. He's starting to good-bye me when I ask if I can say just one more thing. We have an excellent horse coming over for the Japan Cup. Saintly, trained by our master trainer Bart Cummings. It won the Melbourne Cup. It's a very relaxed horse. Sorry, what race did it win? The Melbourne Cup! OK, Tokyo, the tip from Down Under is Saintly.

There, that's done it. Put the mozz right on him. They do the translation of the whole interview when it's finished. I wonder how I sound in Japanese? They are sending me the tape!

That's it, I think I'm nearly through. I might just about last till Stakes Day.

Saturday 9 November. Stakes Day

Miss the dawn chorus, but wake at 6.30 am. Today I've cracked the big invite to Bill's Boot Party. That's the brother-in-law, William, of Hong Kong fame. I'm keen to get there because he touched me for $50 last time we were at the races and he still owes me for the Grand Final tickets. He's a bit down on his luck. Last year he had the big marquee in the nursery car park but I think he is starting to tire of the freeloaders. Real estate hasn't been doing too well, either. So this year it's the boot on the asphalt. My first chance to scab a free lunch. Champagne too. The usual suspects will be there. I ring to confirm. Cancelled! Visiting Malaysian property tycoon!

Oh well, time for a regular Saturday. Do the ratings. Put on The Missus's lucky quaddie at the tote. Spot Jim The Punter. Didja back Saintly? Nah, did you. Nah. And my favourite pensioner, Jack Hunter. What are ya tips, Jack? Well, I've got 50 cents each-way on Prattler, and 50 cents on that horse of Shelley Hancox. What's its name? Kalaring. And I've got a box trifecta on Lochrae, Buzzoff and Rose of Portland. Five blooming bucks! I like Lochrae, Jack, says I. Well, says Jack, at least I got one right.

And I'm off. Another beautiful Melbourne day. I manage to sneak past John Duggan's place without being spotted. I know which direction to go because the blooming blimp is boring straight ahead to the track above me. I'm rushing across the car park, because I've got to get there by the second. You can tell it's public because the corks are plastic. Hey, there's Franco and Mrs Cozzo of Footiscray! I arrive just in time to see the horses hit the parade ring. I rule out Kiwi Golfer, because he doesn't like his lugging bit. Chomping, grinding, trying to spit it out. I'm still learning about bits, and obviously, so is Kiwi Golfer. Ancient Ritual looks older than The Hum. Too Ancient!! I check the race book and find that he's only eight years old, but he looks 20, so I rule him out. A couple of others are showing signs of bad behaviour, so I take a trifecta. It gets up! Nothing nicer than an early strike. I know I'm in for a good day. It doesn't matter what happens now.

I settle in the birdcage. Time for lunch. Now I know, as soon as I reach into my nosebag for the first sandwich that something is going to happen. Sure enough, a horse goes past putting on the whole stallion display. Proud whinny and swish. Be buggered if I'm going to follow him, I just make a note of the strapper and will check him later.

What's a stallion display, you ask? Well, something every apprentice horse watcher should do is visit the Open Day at the Werribee Veterinary School. There, once a year, twice a day, they give a demonstration of semen collection from a stallion. The mare, on heat, is tethered in the centre of the arena, and the stallion led in. He's upright, proud, glossy, tail swished, prancing and whinnying. This looks like it's going to be rape. He's rearing, really showing off. And just when he mounts the mare, and just when you fear the worst, they deflect him into an artificial vagina and capture his semen for other mares. Once you've seen such a performance you don't forget what a stallion display is. Stunning.

He's back. I didn't have to worry about identifying the strapper because he's still going full bore all the way back to his stall. Everybody at Flemington must have heard him by now! I finish my lunch and mosey over. Well, I'll be buggered. It's Lochrae! Favourite for the main race. There's one other bloke looking at him, and he risks a "nice horse" with me. Yeah, looks nice, now. And he did. Settled right down, nearly asleep, excellent looking condition and fitness. He's from the owner's farm. Gives me the good oil. They reckon he'll improve three lengths on his last run. The legs have been a bit of a worry, but OK now. Not worried about him feeling his oats, are ya? Na, na, but he has been a bit of a stallion. Yeah, I saw him before, but he looks OK now.

Saintly appears in the parade ring. First time I've seen him this carnival. Now, there's a relaxed horse!! All drooping long neck and loose strap. The Cup winner's rug covers what we can only assume is magnificent condition and fitness. No wonder he won The Cup.

They are out for the next, the Stakes. There's Lochrae! Oh, no. Bandages! Beautiful cannon bone jobs. Look like hard plaster!! Two faults! I can only rule out one other horse. These are all very nice, well-behaved horses. Greg Miles, the course broadcaster, announces that Lochrae's been backed from 8s to 5s. If that's smart money, they are certainly smarter than I am. Can I make a prediction here? Lochrae can't win. I take a trifecta and lose. But look. Lochrae finished last!

I run into Emil Makiv before the seventh, looking lost, a refugee from Bill's Boot Party. Whaddya like? Super Shaquille. I check my list. It's the only horse I've put a line through. I don't have the heart to tell him. He's had a rotten carnival.

Final score: two trifectas out of five. I feel very smug. To the train. I buy a ticket because I'm ridden with guilt. Besides, police and security staff outnumber racegoers 10 to one. There's Bill Collins, the race caller, looking very frail on a walking stick. Why is he catching the train, I ask the bloke next to me? An Australian racing icon, catching the train? He should be in a limo. And he's so sick. Someone tells me he presented a trophy, too. That's miserable. Aren't the VRC miserable. Surely, if he was the guest of the club, they should send him home in a car? I tell everyone who cares to listen that I'll write a letter to Brian Beattie. I can even sit down in the train. And I don't have to sing.

Monday 11 November

Turn the mobile off and bung it in the bag. Into the university to collect my mail. The Departmental Manager has a heap of papers on his desk, the University News. There's a photograph of me and Phar Lap on the front (Photo 4). Take one, take three, he says. He reckons I'm looking a bit paunchy in the photo. The Head walks in. Why don't we see more of you in Parkville, he enquires. Because you don't pay me, I reply. For 20 years I've been bringing in industry research grants to the university, for what. A photo? We banter a bit, but I resolve to write him a letter. The uni wants to cash in on my fame without kicking in to my kick. I reckon that sucks.

Wednesday 13 November

I write three letters, to all the big bosses. One to Little Johnny, asking him to save the ABC, one to the head of my department, asking him to give me some money, and one to Brian Beattie, to complain about the miserableness of the VRC. I feel much better.

Saturday 16 November. Sandown Cup

Only a few impressions. I'm winding down. Running out, really. There are no mobile phones or suits on the platform at Flinders Street on Sandown Cup day. The carnival is over. The last day of the spring, the last reprise for Cup horses.... From the train I spot the

Photo 4
Phar Lap and Geoffrey. Paunchy?

Ming Wing on the horizon and remember the heady days of Monash and Albert Langer.... Glimpses of red smoke and human beings falling from the sky suggest we're near the track.... I'm about to cough up $10 for a ticket, when a nice lady hands me a complimentary. She must be Marco's sister. I knew he'd come good.

I like Sandown. I think it's the sense that racing gets back to normal. It's always hot, and there's time to relax, freedom to move, to see the horses. Conditions for horse watchers are excellent, with easy stable access and not too far to walk, and nice springy Kikuyu grass to cushion the step. Not so many Muggles round the mounting yard. Have a bet without a hat in line ahead of you. No fear of getting poked in the eye with a feather. A can of VB, only $2.70. Last week it was $3.50!

There's Andrew Peacock, the Kooyong colt, checking his filly saddling Court of Honour. I follow the horse to the ring. It's all head up and swished tail. Compare The Count, relaxed; Few Are Chosen, head up, tugging; Valance, flared tail, uh oh, he's shitting, that's why it's flared; Circles of Gold, OK; Royal Snack, OK; Super Slew, nose roll, lugging bit, plus swish. I hate nose rolls. Cherontessa OK; Seto Bridge, plenty of head action, changing stride; Gaekwar, damn, missed him; Noble Benbara, long shot, head up and swish. A cloudburst for the cup. Watch it on the telly....

I'm standing on the platform at Flinders Street waiting for the Broady train. An old geezer sidles up and asks me what won the last. I tell him the 9, Papal Monarch. What was second? 12. What was third? The 1. Now, how did he know I was a punter?

And the bottom line. Did I win? Over the whole carnival? Well, I'm like most punters. I've had some big wins in my time and I've had some terrible losses, but the bottom line is this. I still have to report to the university each day for work. The day I retire is the day....Sorry, I'm a record in a rut. The bottom line is this....I've had the best carnival, ever.

Wednesday 20 November. Postscript

I'm off to the Community Health Centre to check my health. I've been running on adrenalin, I know. Dr Warwick Anderson slams the cuff on. It'll be through the roof, for sure. I reckon I'm for the high jump. Blood pressure pills for life?

Chapter 5 Picking losers

There are hundreds, perhaps thousands, of ways that a horse can lose a race. Excuses, excuses, and more excuses. Usually they are put forward in that fascinating post-race ritual, described by Desmond Morris in his book *Horsewatching* as the "Why we were beaten ceremony". After a race the trainer, jockey and owners of each of the losing horses form a huddle in the mounting yard and search for an excuse for the horse's dismal performance (Photo 5). Desmond suggests that simple and plain truths are rarely heard during this ceremony - that the horse is no good; that the other horses were better; that the jockey rode a shocker; or that the trainer under-prepared the horse.

Photo 5
Why we were beaten ceremonies,
Caulfield, 23 February 2002.

I am fascinated by these excuses. So much so that, over 20 years ago, I started keeping an excuse file - a folder of newspaper clippings from the weekend race post-mortems. The file bulged out rapidly and alarmingly, and is still in need of constant pruning and culling to keep it in check. Here are the current Top 50 excuses from this file:

1.   The horse was crucified by the handicapper (it had to carry too much weight).
2.   The horse drew a bad marble (barrier).
3.   The horse needed the run/needs a spell.
4.   The horse was backed up too soon/late (needs more/less time between runs).
5.   The horse needs a shorter/longer distance.
6.   The horse got its tongue over the bit/swallowed its tongue.
7.   The horse's saddle slipped/girth strap broke.
8.   The horse lost/sprung a plate.
9.   The horse was hit in the eye by a flying piece of turf.
10.   The horse collapsed/died.
11.   The horse was hit by a seagull.
12.   The horse was struck on the head by another jockey's whip.
13.   The horse bowed a tendon.
14.   The horse pulled a muscle.
15.   The horse was stripped/raced on by another horse.
16.   The horse had a sore foot/was lame/had heat/had filling in a leg.
17.   The horse pigrooted.
18.   The horse was savaged by another horse during the race.
19.   The horse had to be checked when another horse shifted in/out during the race.
20.   The horse struck itself.
21.   The horse jarred up on the hard track/couldn't handle the heavy track.
22.   The horse broke its leg/put its foot in a hole in the track.
23.   The horse was caught flat-footed in the barrier/missed the start by 10 lengths/knuckled over after jumping away.
24.   The horse bolted.
25.   The horse overraced/pulled/got its head up when being restrained by the jockey.
26.   The horse disliked the slow/fast pace.

27. The horse was trapped three wide for the whole race.
28. The horse ran wide on the home turn (and of course memorably, with Billy Idol on Veandercross).
29. The horse was disappointed/blocked for a run.
30. The horse hit the front too soon/can't come from behind.
31. The horse didn't handle the tight turns of Moonee Valley/Canterbury.
32. The horse did not handle the Melbourne/Sydney way of going.
33. The horse tried to jump the crossing (where horses cross the track to reach the training tracks).
34. The horse resented running inside other horses/needs cover in running.
35. The horse was upset by the marching band/Scottish pipe band/rock band/Rhonda Burchmore/skydivers/crowd noise/ thunder and lightning.
36. The horse was distracted by the TV van videotaping the race.
37. The horse sweated up badly/did not like the hot northerly wind.
38. The horse travelled badly/went berserk in the float on the way to the track.
39. The horse was lazy/too keen.
40. The horse was too green/inexperienced/raced erratically/will benefit from the experience.
41. The horse was on heat.
42. The horse needs to be gelded.
43. The horse was off its feed/is an overdoer.
44. The horse had a low red blood cell count/haemoglobin concentration/haematocrit.
45. The horse's champion sire did not reach peak form until he was older.
46. The horse needs a more/less vigorous jockey.
47. The jockey dropped his/her whip.
48. The jockey mistakenly eased the horse down before the finishing post (and of course memorably, with Roy Higgins on Hyperno).

49.   The jockey mistakenly thought something was amiss with the horse and pulled it up.

50.   The jockey fell off (and once memorably, in Western Australia, was paid to fall off).

And still, there are my five very most favourite excuses. In fifth place, just scraping into the prize money, is Kaladan's excuse:

> When the gates flew open in the 1200 metre Potato, Onion and Broccoli Handicap jockey Terry Duckett was not in the saddle.... the explanation of assistant starter Bill Dale for Kaladan not jumping with the field.

And running on the heels of the place getters, in fourth place, is that old-time favourite, the missing lead bag:

> Friday's incident at Grafton involved the heavily backed favourite Costaplenty, who was disqualified after weighing in light. Costaplenty, ridden by the highly rated apprentice Zac Purton, won the race easily despite the saddle slipping. But it was discovered that the towel and pad that go under the saddle and the lead bag had come adrift near the 600 metres. After calling for the bridle, Purton still weighed in two kilograms short of Costaplenty's weight of 57.

In third place is Sunrise Bay's excuse:

> In Adelaide, the Dalmacia Stakes was awarded to the wrong horse. Correct weight was declared on No. 1 My Latin Boy from No. 10 Sunrise Bay. A later examination of the photo finish revealed that Sunrise Bay had won the race.

In second place is Mystic Outlaw's excuse. What a wonderful story:

> Last night's Moonee Valley meeting ended on a sensational note when leading apprentice Rhys McLeod apparently mistook the laps on Mystic Outlaw in the Frequent Flyer Handicap. McLeod started riding Mystic Outlaw along from the 600 metres the first time around and was at least 10 lengths clear of the rest of the field. At the home

turn, with more than a lap to go, McLeod pulled the whip on Mystic Outlaw and, to the roars of the crowd who were well aware of his mistake, was looking around for challengers when he passed the winning post. McLeod began easing his mount down leaving the straight and it was not until the field caught and passed him that he realised something was drastically wrong. Mystic Outlaw, unfancied in the betting at $26, trailed home a distant last.

And the winner is ....The horse has a virus:

> VRC veterinary steward Dr John Bourke said the virus could be classed as an epidemic. The main problem is that the horses affected appear to be doing well in the stable and also working well on the track. It is only when they are asked for a concerted effort in a race that the virus affects them and becomes known. Dr Bourke said in England there was a recognised Unexplained Poor Performance Syndrome. This led to a virology unit being set up to define the significance of virus diseases.

So, you can see, there are all sorts of ways that a horse can lose. And when all else fails, it can have a virus. And 55 ways that horses can lose are probably just the very extreme tip of a very large iceberg. In fact, there are so many ways a horse can lose a race it is a wonder that there can be any winners! But the implications are quite clear for horse watchers. Our original list of 19 variables was totally inadequate to describe the rich diversity of bad behaviour that can be seen at the racetrack. I desperately needed a new list. Now that my 15 minutes of fame had well and truly expired I could go back to work.

I started by tossing out nearly half of the original 19 behaviour and appearance variables and then I added nearly 40 new ones, some from my Top 50. After all, in our pilot study we were forced to include a broad range of variables with the hope of lucking out on one or two that would point to winners. Now that my thinking had been completely turned around I could concentrate solely on bad behaviour and picking losers. I discarded all unnecessary variables. Some of the variables I ditched would cause apoplexy amongst old-style horse watchers, including the top four appearance variables **Horse type, Fatness, Fitness** and **Coat condition**. The reason for discarding these variables is quite straightforward - they simply don't help much with picking losers. I will discuss this decision again in Chapter 7. I also tossed out **Blinkers**, because they are so common, and **Strapper hold** and **Strap length**. However, strapper control is very important in indicating losers, so much so that I needed eight new variables to describe it adequately. I tossed out **Neck angle - jockey up** because it is virtually the same behaviour as **Head position - jockey up**, and **Tracking** was given the flick by the computer.

On 22 March 1997 I started scoring the horses with my new list of 50 variables. On 9 June 1997 I had my first tentative bet on the new system, and on 6 September 1997 I gave up my computer ratings forever. I had finally entered my seventh and final Age of Punting Man. I punt solely on what I see. As I keep telling The Missus and anyone else who will listen, sometimes it is so good it is scary. But more of that later.

My list of variables has now expanded to over 65, and it is still growing. It can be divided into four main groups, according to where I am watching the horses: the birdcage stalls, the parade ring, the mounting yard and the track. So, let us begin in the birdcage. It is time to start watching.

Chapter 6 Back to the birdcage

I always remember the words of the American folk singer, Pete Seeger:

> For 20 years I've played this banjo tune, and I was lazy. I never really learned it right. Along came my younger brother Mike and he just played it so pretty that he put me to shame. I said, "How do you do it?" And he said, "It's nothing more than double thumbing while you're frailing". I said, "Well I've talked about that, but I never knew how to do it". And so, I sat down and followed some of the advice in my own banjo book. And I practised.

I usually have my lunch, heeding Pete Seeger's advice, sitting down in the birdcage, practising, and watching horses and life pass me by. You see some amazing things. I soon realised that there was so much happening here that I needed to suss out each horse in its stall before each race. So after each race is run I generally return to the birdcage and walk past each stall. Obviously my timing won't be perfect and there will be some horses I will miss if they are being unloaded, or are in the urinal, or are being walked, or blood-tested, or are in stalls 91-130 behind the screen at Flemington. But I'd probably end up seeing about 80% of them.

The first thing I look for is if the horse is **Pawing** (Photo 6). This is a fascinating behaviour pattern. I first thought it might be important when I noticed O'Reilly, the favourite in the 1997 Newmarket Handicap, was pawing the ground vigorously and persistently in his stall. The strapper got really peeved and took him off on walking exercise, where he showed signs of arousal, and the strapper needed two hands to control him properly. The horse broke down during the running of the race with a suspensory ligament problem, but would not have won anyway. In another race I noticed the odds-on favourite pawing the ground in the barrier and then running dismally.

Photo 6
Clerk of the course's mount, Pawing,
Moonee Valley, 23 December 2000.

I wondered whether pawing was a stereotypy. Stereotypies are well known in horses and include things like crib-biting and wind-sucking, weaving, pacing, and box-walking. Ethologists (people like me who study animal behaviour) define them as movement patterns which are repetitive, show little variation in form, and have no apparent function. Horse people would use the term "stable vice", but the ethologists don't like this description because it implies that they are bad behaviours and that the horse has a bad character. In fact we don't know much about the cause of these behaviours, and in some cases they may actually help the horse to cope with some sort of environmental problem.

I sent off an email to Paul McGreevy who is Australia's foremost authority on things to do with horse behaviour and lectures in the vet school at Sydney University. He has written a marvellous book called *Why does my horse ..?* So I asked Paul, why does my horse paw the ground before the race? He replied that pawing is a bit tricky. Wild horses paw when digging to get at food, water or a soft substrate for rolling. Pawing is also seen as a sign of frustration in stallions held back from a mare, ponies tied up out of reach of food, and racehorses being made to stand prior to exercise. But it is not clear if pawing in tied-up racehorses is similar to the pawing of feed frustration. He thought it is most likely a redirected behaviour, but suggested that I should contact Frank Ödberg, another horse guru and ethologist at the University of Ghent.

Frank sent a reprint of his first scientific paper, published in 1973, and fortunately in English. He describes pawing thus:

> The horse repetitively rubs the ground over a short distance from front to rear with one of its forelegs, specifically the front part of the hoof. Sometimes the movement is incomplete e.g. the leg is lifted and kept bent in the air or the leg may not touch the ground, and the movement is completed in the air. The hoof may also only move a few centimetres across the ground, and may even remain where it touches the ground so that it resembles a knocking movement.

Frank agreed with the idea of frustration or thwarting of behaviour being the main cause. He pointed out that pawing in racehorses occurs in a conflict situation, when the horse expects something but cannot yet get it or perform it. Thus a racehorse tied up in a stall in the birdcage expects to race, but is unable to do so, and instead we see what is either an intention movement or a displacement activity. Furthermore, if the horse is always locked up in the stable the pawing behaviour could become chronic, and turn into a stereotypy. Whether pawing is a redirected behaviour, an intention movement, a displacement activity or a stereotypy need not concern us. The ethologists can argue about that. The bottom line is that Frank thought that horses that paw frequently are likely to be frustrated, more aroused, and less likely to perform well.

Strappers dislike their horses pawing and generally try to prevent it. They may simply say "No", "Uh, uh" or "Stop it", tap the horse on the chest or flick it with a towel, take it in hand, or give up and take it for a walk. In extreme cases they may hit the horse. I occasionally see horses with chains tied above their knees to discourage the behaviour (Photo 7).

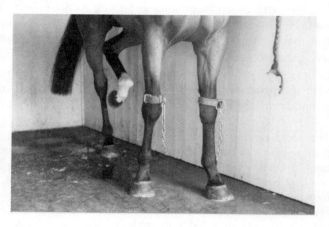

Photo 7
Martial Rule, Pawing chains,
Sandown, 6 March 2002.

Often I may not see pawing, but I will still record it in my race book if I see the telltale sign of scrape marks on bare concrete or a hole in the straw bedding. There is a trend now away from use of straw in the race day stall, with Sandown using rubber mats and Moonee Valley using rubberised bitumen. These surfaces will minimise any possible impact damage through pawing, but make the behaviour harder to detect. And some strappers will try to trick me. They hate any sign of pawing and will carefully replace any straw! I have seen others kick the straw away as soon as the horse arrives. My main conclusion about pawing is that the horse is aroused to some extent, and therefore not completely calm.

Weaving is another stable stereotypy seen in the race day stall. The horse moves its weight from foreleg to foreleg and swings its head from side to side whilst standing in the same place. The behaviour is repeated in a regular and unchanging manner. In the home stable weaving is generally performed with the head hanging over the stable door. I have a fairly loose definition of what I regard as weaving and will include virtually any rhythmic head movement - waving from side to side, bobbing, nodding, or tossing up and down - as well as rocking of the whole body. Paul McGreevy reckons that about one in every 20 thoroughbreds is a weaver, so on an average race day with a card of 100 horses you would expect to see five. Weaving is generally regarded as an abnormal behaviour that has been acquired in response to confinement in the home stable. It is most commonly seen at times of anticipation and excitement, such as the clatter of feed buckets, the arrival of an owner, or other horses. Some stables may try to prevent a horse weaving by installing an anti-weaving bar on the stable door, or by hanging a brick or a bottle in the doorway. However, these methods may lead to further frustration if the horse is unable to perform the behaviour, especially if it helps the horse cope with the stable environment. Jonathon Cooper, an ethologist at the University of Lincoln, has found that weaving can often be alleviated to some extent by putting windows in the stable and opening up views to the surrounding countryside or other stables. If a horse is still weaving in the changed environment of the race day stall it generally indicates that it is a hard case. My main conclusion when I see a weaver, bobber, nodder or tosser is that the horse is aroused to some extent, and therefore not completely calm.

Horses in the birdcage often nibble on the tie-up rope. So much so, that you will notice many ropes protected by pieces of plastic or polyethylene to prevent the horse biting right through. **Nibbling** (Photo 8) can be quite variable and some horses may use only the lips, others the teeth. I include horses that are chewing on the wooden sides of the stall in this category. And in some horses the behaviour can be quite stereotyped, as they pick up the rope, nibble along it for a fixed length, drop it, then pick it up again. I have never seen full-blown crib-biting in the birdcage, where the horse grabs onto a timber fixture with its incisors, pulls back and sucks in air. If I see a nibbler, I regard the horse as being aroused to some extent, and therefore not completely calm.

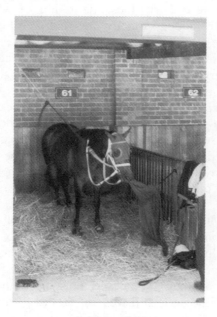

Photo 8
Mendicant, Nibbling a towel,
Caulfield, 2 December 2000.

Whenever I am having my lunch in the birdcage and I hear a loud thump I generally utter an expletive deleted. Usually, bugger. Rarely, but if I've just started on my first sandwich, and gratuitous swearing should not be condoned, bloody hell. I have to get up and find the kicking horse. **Kicking** is when a horse lifts a hind leg and flings it either forwards, sideways or backwards. If it does all three, it is generally called a mule kick! Only rarely have I seen the full-

Photo 9
Paradis, Kicking,
Flemington, 8 November 2001.

blooded, double-barrelled, backwards mule kick (Photo 9). A small
sideways flick with a hind foot is merely a cow kick! I record
kicking regardless of whether the leg makes contact with the rear of
the stall. For example, in Photo 7, Martial Rule is lifting his near
hind leg with the intention of kicking, but doesn't let fly. Kicking can
of course be a very aggressive behaviour, but in the stable
environment it generally indicates mild irritation. You will remember
Taufan's Melody kicking out when Lady Herries tightened the girth
strap (*see* Chapter 1, page 8). One kick is a minor fault; repeated
kicking suggests something more serious. Kicking can be acquired
by a horse as a stable stereotypy and is then repeated constantly in
frustrating situations. If a horse is kicking I regard it as being aroused
to some extent, and therefore not completely calm.

Another home stable stereotypy is box-walking or pacing, where a horse walks repeatedly around a fixed path in its box. At the racetrack the horse is unable to perform this behaviour because it is tied up in the smaller, race day stall. However, some horses may still shows signs of agitation or restlessness, and take small steps sideways, backwards or forwards. I record this as **Restless** behaviour. The horse may or may not be a box-walker in the home stable, but if the horse is not standing still, then the behaviour indicates that it is aroused to some extent, and therefore not completely calm.

Sometimes I will come across a horse in a stall without a strapper. Maybe they've gone for a Tosca, a pie and sauce, or a VB. Maybe even a bet. Or maybe they are in a large stable and are needed to help saddle another horse. Or maybe they are just gasbagging to a mate. I regard all this as a very bad sign and write in my race book **No strapper** (Photo 10). If a horse was weaving or pawing, or showing even greater signs of arousal in the strapper's absence, I would cross it out straight away. The reason for this is that the horse is a highly social animal. I simply assume that for a herd animal, the absence of its closest companion, the human handler, is likely to increase the horse's arousal. Sometimes a trainer will bring two horses to the races, which are entered in different races, but only one strapper. The strapper has to divide his/her time between the two horses. I still write **No strapper** in my race book for the horse standing alone, mainly because I don't have a variable for **Half a strapper**.

In contrast, many trainers are well aware of the social nature of horses and bring a **Pony** (Photo 11) to the races as a companion for their horse. I record this in my race book. The most famous stable pony that I can remember is Shiloh, who accompanied the champion sprinter, Manikato. Bob Hoysted, the trainer of Manikato, has no doubt that Shiloh helped keep his mate calm. Bob was well known for his compassionate care of horses and Shiloh kept going to the races with other Hoysted horses until the grand old age of 35.

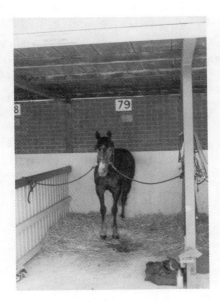

Photo 10
Mighty Ming, No strapper,
Sandown, 25 November 2000.

Humans make good stable ponies, too. In 1974 James Lynch of the University of Maryland Medical School investigated the effects of human contact on heart rate in two horses. The horse's owner (and trainer) approached the horse's stall, stood quietly outside the stall for 2 minutes without speaking to or touching the horse, and then left. In one horse heart rate increased from 33 to 46 beats per minute as the owner approached, then dropped back to 30 beats after about 30 seconds. It increased again when the owner left. If the owner entered the stall and petted the horse on the head and neck, speaking quietly to it, the heart rate dropped below resting levels. In the second horse the owner's approach and exit caused heart rate to increase from 40 beats per minute to 60 to 75 beats per minute. When the owner entered the stall to pet the horse he put his head down, half closed his eyes and stood motionless for the entire time.

Photo 11
Shanassi and Pony,
Sandown, 21 March 2001.

When the owner stood outside the stall the horse repeatedly poked his nose through the bars and paced back and forth in the stall. Obviously, close human contact can have a calming effect on the horse.

A dramatic demonstration of the magnitude of this calming effect has been given by Jane Crawley and Arnold Chamove of Massey University. They looked at the effect of human contact on the abnormal behaviour of four racehorses in full training. They observed the horses at the racetrack when they were tied up in stalls awaiting exercise. They recorded chain chewing, kicking, head nodding and pacing when the horses were *Alone* (no human within 8 metres), when a person stood passively *Beside* the horse within arms' length, but not touching it, and when a person *Touched* the horse, stroking the head and neck. The amount of abnormal behaviour decreased from an average of 24-32 occurrences in five minutes when the horse was *Alone*, to 4-12 when a human was *Beside* the horse, to 0-4 when the horse was being *Touched*.

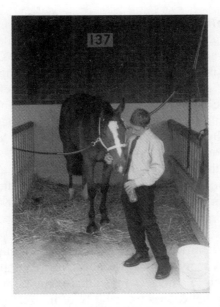

Photo 12
Peri Bingle and Positive Strapper,
Sandown, 17 November 2001.

You now won't be surprised to learn that the final two variables I score in the birdcage are **Hand-held** and **Positive strapper**. I define a horse as hand-held if the strapper is holding it by the leading strap, or if the horse is tied up, holding onto one of the tie-up ropes. If the strapper is touching or petting the horse in any way, including kissing, I write **Positive strapper** in my race book (Photo 12). If the strapper is stroking the withers region of the horse I write **Very positive strapper**! This needs some further explanation.

In the wild, horses live in groups, generally comprised of one stallion, several mares, and their immature offspring. Young bachelor stallions without their own harems also band together in small groups. Various studies of these groups indicate that horses will form strong bonds with other horses of similar age and dominance within the group. They maintain these bonds through mutual grooming. Two horses will stand head to tail and nibble each other with their incisors, generally in the region of the base of the neck. This grooming can have a remarkable calming effect. Claudia Feh and Jeanne de Mazières observed that the preferred grooming site in Camargue horses was the base of the partner's neck, in front of the shoulder blade, and including part of the withers. When horses were scratched by humans in this region they had lower heart rates than horses groomed at a non-preferred site low on the shoulder. They suggested the calming effect was the result of a major ganglion of the autonomic nervous system lying close to the preferred site. Hence, strappers who are aware of this effect get very high commendations in my race book.

When I am in the birdcage I often see something unusual that is not covered by one of my regular variables. An example is a strapper applying a **Twitch** to a horse's lip so that it can be saddled. This is a form of restraint that causes immobility of not just the head, but the whole body. Commercial and homemade twitches can be used, with varying degrees of effectiveness. The principle is to apply pressure to the sensory nerves of the upper lip, near the incisor teeth. The usual explanation for the effectiveness of twitching is that the pain and discomfort it causes diverts the horse's attention while it is being saddled. Other similar techniques of restraint include grabbing and twisting an ear, or pinching and twisting a handful of skin on the neck or behind the shoulder. While a horse can cope with and quickly recover from a short burst of pain, I regard it as a bad sign, and note it in my book. However, in an interesting study of the twitch, Evert Lagerweij and colleagues at the University of Utrecht found that application of a twitch reduced both the heart rate and the behavioural reaction of horses to a painful stimulus, pricking with a sharp needle. They concluded that the twitch may activate some of the mechanisms involved in pain relief, since it appears to induce both analgesia and sedation, and that it may be more akin to acupuncture.

Other examples of things I might see are the chains I mentioned earlier on an inveterate pawer, a fly mask, or a horse being replated, or a trainer applying an ice pack. Or a strapper drinking a can of Bundy and Coke. Or a horse trying to eat its straw bedding. Or a trainer trying to hide his horse in a different stall. Or a strapper switching the horse names above the stall to confuse the humble punter. I have even seen a strapper with a bleeding hand because he had been bitten by his horse! I write all this down, in case it can provide further insight into a horse's state of mind. And you never know, it could even become my next variable, number 66.

And one more other thing. Before leaving the birdcage at Flemington, if you are a feller, make sure you check out the ivy-cloaked Gentlemen's. This used to be the most beautiful urinal on earth. None of your stainless steel or white ceramic here, but ginormous slabs of grey slate. And the best thing was the constant waterfall of running water. If you had a start-up problem, this fixed it for sure. I used to choose the third bay from the left and aimed for a spot below the copperplate signature "David City Steeple 1957". But I regret to report that the VRC has recently installed an automatic flushing system. Is nothing sacred? What is happening to our racing heritage? If you are a party girl, duck in and check out the desecration.

Chapter 7 Perving in the parade ring

The first thing I look at when a horse enters the parade ring is the bit. There are several reasons for this. The first is historical respect. Archaeologists have found evidence of the use of a bit on a horse at a site in the Ukraine dating from 4000 BC. Apparently people were riding horses before the wheel was invented 500 years later, around 3500 BC. The horse came before the cart. I salute antiquity! The second reason is that the bit helps riders steer, slow down and stop their mounts. It is therefore a crucial piece of riding equipment. The basic design has stayed virtually unchanged for centuries - a metal bar, the mouthpiece, attached to rings on either side of the horse's mouth. The bit sits on the horse's tongue and gums, in the gap between the incisors and the premolars, known as the bars. By pulling gently on reins connected to the two side rings the rider exerts sideways and backwards pressure to move the horse's head.

I'm afraid I'm still learning about bits. In fact, I'm still trying to come to terms with the bewildering array of exotic names. There's the German egg butt snaffle, the metal mullen mouth egg butt snaffle, the loose ring, fixed port mouth steel pelham, and don't forget the regular steel kimblewick. The amazing diversity of bits obscures the fact that there are really only three main types - the hackamore, curb and snaffle. The hackamore is essentially a bit that doesn't have a mouthpiece and is used on horses that will not accept a bit or have a tender mouth. I have yet to see one on the racetrack. Curb bits are used by Western riders and come in thousands of shapes and combinations of mouthpieces. They differ from the snaffle in that the mouthpiece usually has a rise in the middle that relieves pressure on the horse's tongue and applies it to the roof of the mouth. Instead of rings on the side they have metal bars or shanks for attachment of the reins. The cheek straps are attached to a

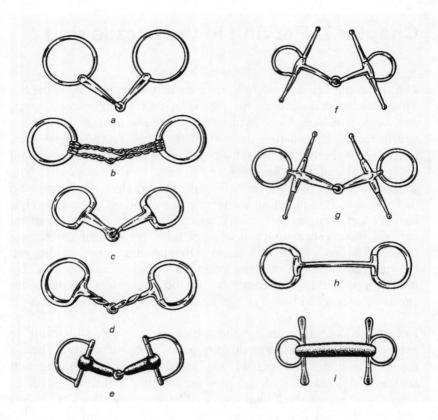

Figure 7.1
Types of snaffle bits: *a*, jointed mouth; *b*, flat ring, Y or W twisted wire snaffle; *c*, jointed mouth, German egg butt snaffle; *d*, jointed mouth, twisted egg butt snaffle; *e*, rubber-covered racing Dee snaffle; *f*, egg butt full cheek snaffle; *g*, Australian loose-ring snaffle; *h*, metal mullen mouth egg butt snaffle; *i*, soft rubber mullen mouth full-spoon cheek snaffle.
Reprinted from Joan duPont, From egg butt to billet strap, The American Quarter Horse Journal, March 1973, p. 85, with kind permission of the publisher.

ring on the top of the shank and the reins to a ring on the bottom. A curb bit gives the rider more leverage when the reins are pulled. I took myself off to the State Library to read Tom Roberts's classic book, *Horse Control and the Bit*. Fortunately, Tom reassured me that racehorse watchers need only concern themselves with snaffle bits. The mouthpiece of snaffle bits is either jointed or straight, with rings for the reins at both ends. There are four main types of ring: round, egg butt, racing Dee, or full cheek. Furthermore, the mouthpiece may be rubber covered for horses with soft mouths. Even so, just considering the possible combinations of joint type, ring design and material, there are at least 16 basic types of snaffle bit. Some types are illustrated in Figure 7.1. In addition, another common horse racing bit is the ring bit or lugging bit, which consists of a simple metal ring attached to the snaffle and prevents the horse hanging in or laying out, or in other words, keeps it running in a straight line.

Photo 13
Mighty Impulse, Soft snaffle and Ring bit,
Flemington, 12 May 2001.

Snaffle bits are generally regarded as mild bits with the severity controlled by the size of the mouthpiece. The smaller the diameter of mouthpiece, the more severe the bit. When the rider pulls on the reins he is pulling directly on the mouth of the horse. The horse's lips can sometimes be pinched by the rings or the rings may pull through the mouth. To prevent these problems racing Dee and egg butt snaffles have a metal casing around the joints and full cheek snaffles have small bars that prevent the rings from sliding into the mouth. Cheekers, small round circles of plastic that fit over the mouthpiece or are incorporated into the bridle, can also reduce the action of the rings on the corners of the mouth. When I record **Bit type** in my race book I assume every horse has a regular snaffle bit, unless I see something different. I will make a note if a horse has a **Ring bit**, a **Ring bit** with **Soft** snaffle (Photo 13), a **Soft** rubber bit, or **Cheekers** (Photo 14).

Photo 14
Born Brave, Cheekers,
Moonee Valley, 5 May 2001.

The most unusual bit I have encountered would be the snake bit worn by the three-year-old filly My Jaspa when she won at Caulfield on 3 April 1999. I still don't know what it looked like because, aside from my aversion to snakes in the mouth, I was distracted by all the other control devices the horse required, including a tongue tie, pacifiers, and the assistance of the clerk of the course. Also, according to the

Victoria Racing Club's *Regulations*, snake bits, aluminium bits, basket bits and Tom Thumb bits are not permitted. So I don't know how My Jaspa's trainer got away with it. Although I don't place a great deal of importance on bit type, I still record it assiduously as my first parade ring variable in order to focus my mind and my attention straight away onto the horse's mouth and ensure that I have my pen at the ready next to the horse's name in the race book.

The bridle is probably less important for horse watchers since its main job is simply to hold the bit correctly in the mouth and to stay securely attached to the horse's head. The simplest type of bridle consists of a leather headband that passes across the back of the horse's head behind the ears and is buckled to cheek straps on either side. A throat strap joins the headband below the ears, and a brow band joins each side of the headband in front of and just below the ears. The cheek straps loop onto the rings of the bit, together with the reins. The bit should rest firmly and evenly in each corner of the mouth so that the skin forms one or two wrinkles. If the bit is too low in the mouth the horse may play with it or get its tongue over the bit.

Occasionally a horse may wear a martingale. Fixed martingales are banned under the Victoria Racing Club's *Rules of Racing*. They are a strap from the noseband to girth, supported by a neck strap, intended to stop a horse carrying its head too high. A running martingale is a leather strap attached to the girth, which runs between the front legs and divides into two straps with rings, through which the reins pass. Its job is to direct the pull from the reins downwards and backwards onto the bit. In our pilot study we observed it once in 867 horses. This is too rare for it to be a useful variable.

There seems little doubt that pulling on the reins causes intense discomfort. While most horses get used to the bit, some resist and fight against it. If a bit is not properly adjusted the horse can lift and pull back its tongue, pushing the bit back onto the first premolar teeth. The bit cannot go any further backwards because of the fleshy corners of the mouth. The horse grips the bit tightly between the teeth and bites on it. This is of course known as champing at the bit. If the horse was being ridden and succeeds in getting "the bit between its teeth", the rider has no control and the horse may do a Harold Holt. I do not record champing as such, because it implies that the horse is keen to move forward. I simply note instead whether the horse is **Chewing**, that is moving its jaws rapidly up and down, with the mouth open, or **Grinding**, showing less jaw movement, but making a grinding noise clearly audible up to a distance of about 2 to 5 metres. Horses appear to show their resentment of the bit in several ways. Grinding may be one, and chewing another. **Gaping** could possibly be a third. This is when the mouth is open to a considerable degree, and often accompanied by sideways displacement of the lower jaw, known as crossing the jaws. On two occasions I have seen a horse gaping and with the ring bit stuck on its front incisors in an apparent attempt to escape the action of the bit. The horses in Photos 13, 15, 17, 18, 42, 53, 54 and 56 are all gaping.

Photo 15
Jet Star, Neck twisted and Gaping,
Moonee Valley, 24 March 2001.

I record another behaviour which I call **Neck twisted**, when the horse extends its neck forwards, often twisted or rotated to one side, often accompanied by gaping, and ears pointing to the sides or backwards (Photo 15). The horse appears to be straining and reaching forwards into the bit. A horse can also avoid the action of the bit by arching its neck and pivoting its head downwards from the poll, with its mouth open. I record this as **Neck arched** (Photo 16). The horse often appears to be attempting to escape from the action of the bit by relieving pressure on the bars and corners of the mouth.

Photo 16
Woodpecker, Neck arched,
Flemington, 12 May 2001.

A horse may sometimes get its tongue over the bit, which will interfere with the steering and control of the horse, and also its breathing. Some horses can also pull their tongues back so that the bit is resting directly on the bars of the mouth, which can be uncomfortable for the horse and cause bruising. In extreme cases a horse can swallow its tongue or "choke down". Often, when a racehorse has an inexplicable failure, the trainer will assume that it is a tongue problem and try using a **Tongue tie** (Photo 17) at the next start. This can be a tricky task, since grabbing hold of a horse's tongue is like catching a fat, slippery eel. Various materials are used, but commonly a strip of crepe bandage about 25 mm wide is looped around the tongue and tied under the jaw behind the bottom lip. The bandage must be tight enough to prevent the horse from retracting its tongue, but not so tight that it cuts off circulation. Rubber bands and panty hose are also commonly used.

Photo 17
Lava Lady, Tongue tie,
Moonee Valley, 5 May 2001.

Victoria Racing Club *Rule of Racing 93* states:

> Any bit and/or attachments or additional gear not generally used including tongue-tie, bandages and boots shall not be worn by a horse in any race without the approval and permission of the Stewards. Any such gear approved and used on a horse in a race shall continue to be used on that horse without variation until permission to remove or vary the same has been obtained from the Stewards.

Approved gear changes are recorded in the race book and generally announced over the public address system by the course broadcaster. However, tongue ties are often difficult to observe, especially if the material is a dark colour, such as black panty hose. And since they will only be noted in the race book if the horse has not worn one previously, it is important to look carefully. Most horses will quietly tolerate a tongue tie, but if it is not tied correctly the horse may resent it, and even bite on the tongue. On several occasions I have seen a tongue tie removed in the mounting yard before a race. Signs of resentment are probably similar to those seen in resentment of the bit. But the most dramatic sign of resentment is when a horse literally spits the dummy. Pennywort spat out its rubber band tongue tie in the mounting yard, right at my feet, before Race 6 at Caulfield on 18 May 2002. Surprisingly, the trainer ignored this forceful sign of indignation, and refitted it. Pennywort, the $3.00 favourite, and carrying about $95,000 in win bets, finished sixth of the nine runners.

Photo 18
St Christoph, Lolling,
Moonee Valley, 24 March 2001.

I record two further behaviours related to the tongue, **Lolling** and **Licking**. Lolling (Photo 18) is when the tongue is hanging out of one side of the mouth, either with or without a tongue tie. Lolling in itself is probably not a bad behaviour, but in conjunction with other signs of bit resentment could indicate a poor performance. Some horses race quite successfully with a lolling tongue. My favourite used to be

Star Binder, who virtually dragged his tongue along the track when racing. Licking is also a relatively benign behaviour. I record any repeated protrusion of the tongue as licking. Licking is regarded as a sign of submission in many animals and horses will, like dogs, repeatedly protrude their tongues when being petted.

I wrote off to the prominent American veterinarian and horse wrangler Robert M. Miller to ask his views on mouth behaviour of the horse in response to the bit. He regards playing with the bit and tongue lolling as "displacement behaviour" and an indication that the horse is stressed. He regards "mouthing" of the bit, when the horse licks its lips and chews, as normal submissive behaviour in response to control of movement. Horses will do this whether or not a bit is in their mouths. Robert also tried to sell me a copy of his book and video *Understanding the Ancient Secrets of the Horse's Mind*. I suppose I'd better send off for them. I'm a sucker for anything that has the word "secret" in its title.

Putting an object in a horse's mouth causes it to salivate. I record **Salivating** on a scale of 1 to 3. 1 indicates saliva is visible, mainly at the corners of the mouth; 2 indicates considerable salivation, which may be frothing up; and 3 indicates saliva or froth is dripping from the horse's mouth. A horse cannot breathe and swallow at the same time, so it has to stop breathing to swallow excess saliva, or it may choke. I therefore assume that excessive salivation is a bad sign (Photo 19).

Before moving on from salivation, we must pause for a minute's silence, and pay our respects to Vic Rail, trainer of the mighty front-runner, Vo Rogue. Vic was infamous for his worn visage and dropped chest. I remember encountering him once playing blackjack at Jupiter's casino. He wanted to double a bet and reached into his pocket to pull out more chips. A whole heap of black $100 chips fell to the floor, and I watched as Vic scrabbled around picking them up. There lie the winnings of the mighty Vo, thought I. Unfortunately Vic contracted the Hendra virus, most probably from ingestion of

Photo 19
Sun Eagle, Salivating,
Flemington, 27 February 2002.

horse saliva. Vale Vic! And so when you see horse saliva, remember Vic, and remember, flying horse spittle can be dangerous. Hey, horse watchers, be careful out there!

I record any major modifications to the bridle, in particular the use of a **Crossover noseband**. This is a device which is used to prevent the horse evading the action of the bit by opening its mouth. In the most common type the front strap passes in front of the bit (Photo 20). I also note whether the horse has a **Nose roll** or shadow roll. This is a large fluffy doodad, generally made of wool, and often brightly coloured (Photo 21). I have come across several explanations for the apparent function of the nose roll. One is that it stops the horse shying at shadows by restricting its downward vision. Another is that it forces horses that carry their heads up to lower them, and presumably race more generously. And a third is that it softens the edge of the horse's visual field. I have a strong personal aversion to nose rolls, but I have to admit that they haven't hindered some horses. Vintage Crop and Kingston Rule are two Melbourne Cup

Photo 20
Grand Seattle, Crossover noseband and Ear flicking,
Moonee Valley, 5 May 2001.

Photo 21
Kurtray, Nose roll and Salivating,
Flemington, 16 December 2000.

horses that have carried nose rolls to victory. You may also occasionally see **Side winkers**. These are also fluffy doodads attached to the cheek strap of the bridle, which probably act in the same way as conventional blinkers by restricting rearward vision.

Photo 22
Darting Princess, Pacifiers,
Flemington 16 December 2000.

After looking at the mouth, tongue and nose I check out the eyes. I no longer record if a horse is wearing blinkers, but I do note mesh eye protectors or **Pacifiers**. These are the tea strainers, generally made of a metal or plastic mesh, fitted into a hood over the horse's head (Photo 22). They were invented by the Brisbane jockey, Michael Pelling, and reputedly have a calming effect on horses. They are often used on horses that tend to get a little bit stirry or fired up, and often quieten them quite considerably. The mesh will also protect the horse's eyes from flying lumps of turf. In Melbourne they are generally banned if the track is rated slow or heavy, on the grounds that flying mud could completely restrict the vision of a horse in pacifiers. Even on good tracks I have noted horses in pacifiers returning to the mounting yard with much of the mesh clogged with pieces of grass. It is easy to miss pacifiers if they are incorporated into a hood fitted with blinkers. The former Bart Cummings-trained Typhoon is a good example of a horse that was often difficult to handle wearing pacifiers to good effect.

Earmuffs are another interesting piece of equipment, which have recently made their debut on Melbourne racetracks (Photo 23). Apparently they are meant to prevent the horse hearing the sound of other horses during a race. I'm not sure how effective they would be since they are made of a fairly thin rubber/foam material. They look like something Annette Funicello would have worn in the Mickey Mouse club, but I'll need to see more before passing judgement.

Photo 23
Our Bullbaa, Earmuffs,
Caulfield, 1 April 2002.

Finally, I record the horse trainer's favourite indicator of temperament, **White eye** (Photo 24). There is a general suspicion amongst horse people that horses showing a lot of white in their eyes are as mad as cut snakes. Of course some horses may have a genuine walleye, where the iris lacks the normal pigment and is either white or pale blue in colour (Photo 25). This lack of pigment in the iris does not interfere with normal vision. The most prominent walleyed

Photo 24
Classic Benbara, White eye and Ears back,
Moonee Valley, 24 March 2001.

Photo 25
Logical Reason and Walleye,
Moonee Valley, 3 February 2001.

horse racing in Melbourne in recent times has been the wonderfully named Eye Wonder. But when I see the whites of a horse's eye, I note it down. I don't know whether these horses are trustworthy or not. But I did notice that a prominent human, the NSW Olympics Minister Michael Knight, showed plenty of white below his iris when interviewed on television. Would you trust him?

And one more thing on temperament of horses. If you ever have an idle moment let your eye wander to the hair whorl on the face of a horse. It was reported in the 1960s that there appeared to be a relationship between the position of the whorl and temperament. Surprisingly, this is not as hair-brained as it sounds. In humans, scalp hair patterning is determined during weeks 10-16 of foetal development and can serve as a permanent marker of abnormal brain development. For example, schizophrenics are more likely to have anti-clockwise whorls than normal people. Roxanne Barker has reported that quarter-horse trainers are well aware of the importance of hair whorl location. The higher the whorl, the "hotter", or more highly strung, is the horse. Horizontal positioning is apparently also important. If the whorl is left of centre, looking at the horse's face, the horse is more insecure. If it is right of centre it is more independent and aggressive. In cattle Temple Grandin has shown that cattle with high hair whorls are more likely to panic when restrained than cattle with low hair whorls.

Intriguing as all this is, I'm afraid that I'm generally too busy to include **Hair whorl position** as one of my variables. Also, as you may know, I tend to treat appearance and conformation variables with some disdain. If I do see a horse with a high right whorl, I don't immediately regard it as a convicted criminal. I'll give the horse an even break and suss out its temperament by observation of its behaviour. And besides, the blinker hood will obscure observation of the whorl in 40% of horses.

From the head, I drop my eyes to look at the horse's legs and feet. I'm looking for **Boots and bandages**. I've always been wary of horses racing in bandages since I read Rem Plante's dire warnings in his 1970s classic *Australian Horse Racing and Punters' Guide*. Plante was unequivocal:

> It is a notorious fact that many horses carrying bandages in a race are not running true to form. If a horse needs bandages for one reason or another, it is not fit to race. Apart from having sore legs, the bandages may be applied too tightly which would affect the horse's action.

Plante's only exception was horses that always wear bandages, which may protect them from hitting themselves.

The boots and bandages expert is Ian Wright, at the University of Cambridge. I'll attempt to briefly summarise his wisdom here. There are three main types of injuries that a horse can inflict upon itself. Brushing injuries occur when the supporting limb is struck by its advancing partner, and are mainly confined to the region of the fetlock and lower cannon. Speedycutting injuries are so called because they occur during fast work and are found in the upper cannon area. Over-reaching injuries are generally cuts produced by the toe of an advancing hind foot on the back of the forelimb on the same side. Various boots and bandages are used to prevent these interference injuries:

Brushing boots are generally rectangular in shape with a bump on the bottom to cover the inside of the fetlock. They protect the cannon, splint bone and fetlock. They are usually made of leather or plastic, with a padded lining, and secured with three or four straps and buckles. I have seen them mainly on hurdlers and steeplechasers, and only rarely on flat racehorses (Photo 26). **Speedycutting boots** are similar to brushing boots, but only provide protection above the fetlock. I see them only rarely too. Bohemiath wore speedycutting boots in the 2000 Melbourne Cup.

Exercise bandages are used primarily to protect the foreleg flexor tendons from over-reach injuries. They don't prevent these injuries

Photo 26
Jet Star, Brushing boots,
Moonee Valley, 24 March 2001.

as well as boots, but conform better to the shape of the foreleg, which is important in horses in fast work. Most trainers believe that these bandages also provide some support to the tendons. Ian Wright reckons that this is difficult to justify since the mechanical load applied to these tendons is axial, in other words in the long axis of the limb, whereas the bandage pressure is at right angles to this. Exercise bandages are generally made of crepe, cotton or elasticised cotton. They are applied over a material such as foam rubber or cotton wool and usually cover the cannon from fetlock to knee (Photo 27). They should be tight enough not to slip, but not so tight that they affect circulation of either the underlying skin or tendons. The *Rules of Racing* require bandages to be stitched the full length on the outside of the leg in a contrasting thread.

There have been a couple of absolutely amazing studies of bandages. Kevin Keegan and various vets at the University of Illinois implanted strain gauges into the suspensory ligaments of nine horses. They then measured the strain on the ligament while the horses were standing and walking with various types of casts and supportive bandaging materials, as well as different bandaging techniques. Their results clearly showed that there was no effect of any bandage or bandaging technique on suspensory ligament strain. In another study M.M. Morlock and a mob of mates measured the pressure on the skin under bandages of different materials. They found that some bandages exhibited forces and pressures that might restrict blood flow. Quite clearly, if the intention of bandaging is to provide support for the suspensory ligaments or tendons, then the tension which must be applied increases the risk of restricting blood flow.

Photo 27
Rubison, Cannon bandages and Prancing,
Flemington, 16 December 2000.

Exercise bandages that cover the fetlock area only are generally referred to as **Tapes** and protect the horse's bumpers from abrasion (Photo 28). If you look at a horse with tapes when it returns to the mounting yard after racing you will generally notice that they are

Photo 28
Unknown horse, Tapes,
Sandown, 21 March 2001.

grass stained or dirty where the horse has got down on its bumpers while galloping. Octagonal was a well-known carrier of tapes.

In summary, I note in my race book if a horse is wearing boots or bandages by recording the number of bandages and their location. Hence 2FCB is two front **Cannon bandages** or boots, 4BB is four bumper bandages or **Tapes**. If I see a bandage in any other location I note OB, for **Other bandage** (Photo 29). This may be an elasticised support bandage on a hock, much like worn out 30 year-old footballers may wear on their ankles or knees, or it may be a bandage protecting an old war wound. Whenever I see an OB I usually think of Rem Plante and wonder whether the horse is fit to race.

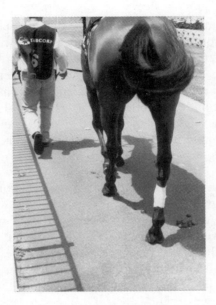

Photo 29
Another Chance, Other bandage,
Sandown, 20 January 2001

Before I leave the parade ring, it is worth commenting on one other piece of equipment, the **Girth strap**. Current practice for fitting a saddle prior to racing is simply to tighten the girth to a tension that does not allow the saddle to slip. Most trainers and strappers learn about this through trial and error. The usual tension applied to keep a saddle on a racehorse is about 13 kg. J.R. Bowers and Ron Slocombe at Melbourne University have recently reported that girths tighter than 10 kg strain reduced horse performance during exercise tests on a treadmill. This is a fascinating result as it suggests that a simple way to pull up a horse would be to overtighten the girth. I am not sure how this knowledge can help horse watchers, since it is virtually impossible to tell, simply by looking at a horse, the tightness of the strap. One possibility is to examine horses after the race and look for telltale signs of pressure marks under the girth. Another possibility is to pay more attention to the sex of the strapper. Bowers and Slocombe also found that female strappers were less heavy-handed than men, and were less likely to overtighten the girth. Girth tensions were on average 2 to 3 kg less when put on by females. This may reflect physical differences in the strength of male and female strappers, or it could also reflect the psychological approach of the individual to the task of applying the saddle and girth. At the moment I do not write **Strapper sex** in my race book, but I'm seriously thinking about it.

Finally, as I have already remarked, I do not record body condition of horses. Most mounting yard watchers probably won't believe me when I say this. And I suppose if a horse is first or second up from a spell I would ever so briefly cast my eye over it for fatness and fitness. But for the casual racegoer, assessing fatness and fitness by visual appraisal is extremely difficult, and takes a lot of practice. And even with a lot of practice it is quite likely that the magnitude of the changes you are trying to detect will be undetectable. Consider the fascinating paper published by R.G. Westervelt and colleagues at Cornell University, New York, over 25 years ago. Westervelt used an ultrasound to measure fat thickness at three sites, the shoulder, rib and rump, before and after exercise. After 90 days of exercise body weight of the horses was unchanged, but fat thickness had declined 4.6 mm at the shoulder, 1.0 mm at the rib, and 3.6 mm at the rump. I defy any mounting yard watcher to detect a change in fat cover over the ribs of less than 1 millimetre when evaluating a horse at two-week intervals between racing. Quite clearly, your time will be better spent detecting easily observable differences in mental attitude and behaviour.

However, if you remain unconvinced, and are keen to give it a go, I suggest that you first try looking at horses away from the racetrack so that you can get to feel them with your hands and fingers as well. And then have another look at Patricia Ellis's guide to condition scoring of horses (*see* Figure 2.3 on page 22).

Chapter 8 Did someone say sex?

I'm sorry, but every now and then, and in every good story, **Sex** rears its ugly head. Lochrae's inglorious last in the 1996 Stakes is one example. Although sex is rarely observed, it is well worthwhile for the horse watcher to have a basic working knowledge of sexual behaviour. My philosophy is that it's best to be prepared. You never know when it might come in handy.

Horses are seasonal breeders that come into oestrus in response to increasing daylight. Oestrus (or heat) is simply a behavioural state which corresponds with ovulation. Ovulation, the shedding of an egg by an ovary, occurs about 24 to 36 hours before the end of heat. If conception does not occur then a mare will ovulate again about 21-22 days later.

Stephanie Tyler has observed the oestrus cycles of free-ranging horses in the New Forest, Hampshire, England. Mares commenced cycling in March and continued through until September. Foals were born in early summer and most mares bred and conceived on the foal heat. The foal heat usually began several days after a mare had foaled and lasted for up to a week. If breeding did not occur during the foal heat or the mare failed to conceive, then oestrus recurred about every three weeks throughout the spring and summer. The length of oestrus was quite variable, but on average was seven days. In one 15-year-old mare it was five weeks. The gestation period of the mares was 11 to 11.5 months.

The breeding season of the mare in the southern hemisphere was first worked out in a seminal study by Virginia Osborne at the University of Sydney in 1966. Virginia collected 6763 reproductive tracts and ovaries from the entire intake of mares to a Sydney horse abattoir over a four-year period. She is truly worthy of a horse watcher's gold medal for devotion above and beyond the call of duty. Each ovary was examined for signs of recent ovulation. The results of her colossal effort are shown in Figure 8.1.

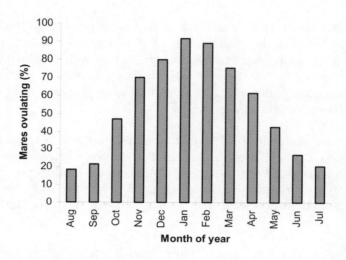

Figure 8.1
Natural breeding season of mares in Australia, shown as the number of mares ovulating each month of the year.
Data from V.E. Osborne, An analysis of the pattern of ovulation as it occurs in the annual reproductive cycle of the mare in Australia, 1966, Australian Veterinary Journal 42, 149-154.

If the breeding season is defined as when at least 50% of the mare population is cycling then the Australian season runs from about mid-October through to late April. The peak of the season is in January/February. In four of Virginia's weekly samples in February she found 100% of mares were ovulating. However, imposed on top of the natural breeding season is the arbitrary establishment of the August 1 birth date for all horses. This birth date ignores the biological clock of horses, so that the stud breeding season starts in advance of the normal breeding season. Stud breeding generally commences on September 8 and finishes on December 31. It is not surprising to find that there is a low level of success obtained from stud matings early in the season. The *Australian Stud Book* statistics for 2000 show that 1287 stallions covered 26,188 mares. The number of live foals born was 16,946, or 64.7% of mares mated.

Figure 8.1 is very important for horse watchers, since it indicates the probability of observing a filly or mare on heat. In winter and early spring, it is a long shot and highly unlikely. In high summer, January and February, it is odds on and highly likely. In autumn and late spring, an even money bet. Since sexual motivation can interfere with performance it pays to be especially vigilant in fillies and mares races at certain times of the year.

In contrast to the seasonal pattern of oestrus behaviour in mares, stallions are sexually responsive throughout the year, but will show peak sexual behaviour in the summer and autumn. K.F. Dowsett of the University of Queensland collected semen from 168 stallions over a four-year period, a silver medal effort. Semen volume, sperm concentration and the total number of sperm in the ejaculate tended to be higher in summer and autumn. A study by S.W. Byers of seasonal variation in the concentration of testosterone, the male sex hormone, confirmed this pattern (Figure 8.2). Testosterone concentrations were highest in summer, with a secondary, smaller increase in the autumn. Dowsett firmly believed that the official breeding season in Australia should be extended for at least two months, or alternatively, the season should start on November 8 and continue at least until the end of February.

When a mare is pregnant or fails to show the cyclical recurrence of oestrus she is said to be in anoestrus. In the northern hemisphere more than 50% of mares are probably in seasonal anoestrus during winter. In Australia the lowest incidence of oestrus occurs after the time of the winter solstice (June 22). Thus, it is still possible to observe a cycling mare in the winter (June till August), but in fewer than 20% of mares. In two of Virginia Osborne's samples in July no

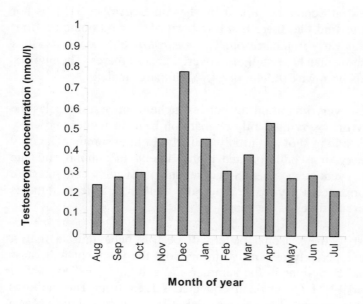

Figure 8.2
Seasonal changes in testosterone concentration in three stallions.
Data from S.W. Byers, K.F. Dowsett and T.D. Glover, Seasonal and circadian changes of testosterone levels in the peripheral blood plasma of stallions and their relation to semen quality, 1983, Journal of Endocrinology 99, 141-150.

mares were ovulating. Winter oestruses tend to be of longer duration than spring, summer and autumn. Dowsett found that the average duration of oestrus was 9.3 days in winter, compared with 6.6 days in summer, 7.5 days in autumn, and 8.2 days in spring. The average length of dioestrus (the time between consecutive heats) was 16.6 days and did not vary with season.

The age of puberty, or sexual maturity, in horses is variable. Stephanie Tyler found that some free-ranging mares came into their first oestrus at 14 to 15 months old, but only 1% foaled at two years old and 13% at three years old. Sexual behaviour was seen in young colts, with full erections of the penis observed in two- to three-month-old colts when they were resting, play-fighting or grooming filly foals. But the age at which a colt first achieved copulation varied from 15 months to almost three years. Thoroughbred fillies have their first oestrus at about 16 to 17 months. Caroline Argo and her assistants at Liverpool John Moores University took needle biopsies from the testicles of Welsh Mountain pony colts at monthly intervals (oooooooooh, ouch, ouch!) to work out when they first started producing sperm. They concluded that puberty occurred between 17 and 19 months, so that at the onset of the two-year-old season all colts were fertile. Puberty in thoroughbred colts is generally regarded as developing between 17 and 22 months. Since the first two-year-old races of the season don't commence until about mid-October, nearly 27 months after the official date of birth for all horses, it can be safely assumed that all horses seen at the racetrack are sexually mature.

A horse watcher's first sex-related task is to look for behavioural signs of oestrus in fillies and mares. Both female and male horses will adopt a typical straddled posture for urination, primarily to avoid wetting their hind legs. A mare would normally urinate only three or four times per day, but when she is in season she could urinate up to 20 times per hour. She stands with her tail raised and displaced to one side, and hind legs slightly apart. She may slightly raise one or both hind legs so that only the toe of the hoof is touching the ground. Urination is followed by repeated protrusion of her clitoris through the vulval lips. This display is known as clitoral winking. The standing oestrus posture can be seen in free-ranging horses both when there is no stallion nearby and when a stallion is in close proximity.

In the early stages of oestrus a mare may be aggressive and non-receptive towards the approaches of a stallion. She may react by kicking, threat posturing, biting, squealing or clamping her tail down firmly. As the mare gets closer to full oestrus she becomes more receptive to close interaction with the stallion and normal copulation occurs. The pre-mating behaviour of both free-ranging horses and thoroughbreds can be remarkably brief. Stallions will generally rush over to a mare that has just urinated and sniff the urine on the ground or her genital region. They will then show the flehmen response (*see* page 113) and may whinny or snort excitedly whilst sniffing her. The stallion may then nibble and lick her rump and hind legs, and show erection of his penis. He then mounts her and after several pelvic thrusts achieves intromission and ejaculation occurs shortly after. Intromission lasts about 30 seconds, and the whole procedure, from stallion approach to dismount, can be less than 60 seconds.

Detection of oestrus in fillies and mares is normally done at a stud farm using a teaser stallion. Mares are exposed to the stallion so that they have visual and olfactory contact, but copulation is not possible. A scoring system for detecting oestrus, similar to one developed by Cindy McCall, at the University of Connecticut, is sometimes used. Mares are given a behavioural oestrus score from 0 through to 4:

0   Rejection of stallion, kicking, squealing, or striking
1   Indifference to stallion
2   Interest in stallion, alert posture, raised tail and urination
3   Increase interest, raised tail, urination and clitoral winking
4   Extreme interest, raised tail, profuse urination, winking,
     and squatting.

Detecting oestrus at the racetrack without a teaser stallion is much harder, but not impossible. The main signs to look out for are a raised tail and urination. If a mare baulks I pay special attention to see if she then urinates. Several times I have seen mares urinate as they are walking, but it can be very difficult to detect. I regret to report that I have yet to observe clitoral winking at the racetrack, but I am ever vigilant, and keep a constant and close lookout. There is no doubt that being on heat can interfere with performance. It is an excuse that is regularly used by trainers to explain inexplicable failure. For example, coming into season and getting her tongue over the bit were advanced as reasons for the failure of the champion mare Sunline in the 1999 Hong Kong Cup.

Observing sexual behaviour in colts and stallions is much easier. Consider the remarkable observations of M. Tischner, from the Institute of Applied Animal Physiology in Krakow, Poland, published in the *Journal of Reproduction and Fertility*. Dr Tischner observed continuously for seven days the frequency and duration of full erection and attempts at masturbation in seven stallions while they were in the stable. During the night a flashlight was used to aid observation. He compiled some amazing statistics, which are surely deserving of a horse watcher's bronze medal. On average a stallion had 7.4 erections per day, a full erection 3.8 times, and attempted to masturbate 4.1 times. The stallions spent a total time of 38 minutes per day with an erect penis, of which 19.5 minutes were spent trying to masturbate. Individual attempts to masturbate lasted approximately four to five minutes. The peak in erection activity was between 0700 and 1000 hours, which may strike a chord in human males familiar with the phenomenon of early morning arousal.

According to Sue McDonnell, an agricultural scientist and expert in sexual behaviour of horses at the University of Pennsylvania, masturbation is a normal behaviour often observed in the resting stallion. Spontaneous erection involves extension of the penis from the prepuce and engorgement to its full length and rigidity. During masturbation the stallion swings his erect penis forwards and rhythmically bounces, presses or slides it against his belly. Ejaculation occurs rarely. Sue found a much higher frequency of erection and masturbation than Dr Tischner, with an average of 18 erections per day in stabled horses. About 75% of erections included masturbation. About 83% of masturbation episodes included "bounces", 57% included "presses" and only 13% included pelvic thrusts. When the horse was bouncing or thrusting his penis his facial expression usually suggested pleasure and contentment similar to that seen during solitary grooming. Occasionally, a trance-like, glazed eye appearance was seen. Ejaculation was observed only four times in 447 erections.

Masturbation in horses has traditionally been regarded as an abnormal, aberrant behaviour, similar to other stable vices such as cribbing or weaving. It was thought to be the product of stable inactivity, regimentation and boredom. It has also been regarded as an expression of frustration and thwarted access to heterosexual activity. However, Sue McDonnell points out that it is commonly observed in feral horses, in both harem stallions and bachelor stallions, and in horses maintained in paddock-breeding conditions. Even breeding stallions maintaining high levels of heterosexual activity have masturbated at rates of up to 10 times per day. Spontaneous erection and masturbation are also seen in geldings, but in general at about half the frequency observed in entire stallions. Sue has concluded that spontaneous erection and masturbation are normal and frequent behaviours in stallions and geldings. They appear to reflect contentment rather than frustration or boredom. She believes that they should not be discouraged in horses.

Whilst investigating this rather indelicate matter of horse masturbation I came across some information that needs to be passed on to punters in the interests of occupational health and safety. N.D. Citron and P.J. Wade, surgical registrars at two London hospitals, reported on several disturbing cases involving penile injuries to humans caused by, of all things, vacuum cleaners. In one case a 60-year-old man said that he was changing the plug of his Hoover Dustette vacuum cleaner in the nude while his wife was out shopping. The machine "turned itself on" and caught his penis, causing severe lacerations. In another case a 65-year-old railway signalman bent down to pick up his tools and caught his penis in a vacuum cleaner, which happened to be switched on. Extensive lacerations to the glans were repaired with catgut with a good result. In a third case a 49-year-old man was vacuuming his friend's staircase in a loose-fitting dressing gown. When intending to switch the machine off he leaned across to reach the plug. At that moment his dressing gown became undone and his penis was sucked into the vacuum cleaner. Quite clearly, vacuuming in the nude is a hazardous occupation with the potential to cause severe trauma. Punters, please take care.

But back to horses. Stallions in racing stables are generally trained not to exhibit sexual behaviour when exposed to mares during work or racing. Interest in mares, erection, masturbation and even penis drop can be actively discouraged by a verbal or physical reprimand. Fortunately, some of the devices available to control masturbation, such as stallion rings, brushes, and nasty-looking spike pads, are rarely used.

The fate of many colts is the unkind cut. Castration is generally carried out prior to puberty. However, it can be done post-puberty if there is little breeding value and stallion-like behaviour, especially aggression, appears to be interfering with handling or performance. Scott Line at the University of California, Davis, found no behavioural differences between male horses castrated as adults or juveniles, with about 5% of geldings continuing to be aggressive towards humans in a stallion-like manner. However, a surprising finding was that sexual behaviour persisted in over 30% of geldings, ranging from the flehmen response, to erection and masturbation, and in some cases, mounting and intromission.

The flehmen response is interesting. **Flehmen** is a German word introduced in the 1930s to describe the dramatic facial grimace of the male horse. It is also known as the "lip curl" or "horse laugh" and is a weird and wonderful behaviour. Flora Lindsay of the Veterinary Anatomy Department at the University of Glasgow has given a complete description of the behaviour, which involves head, neck, lip, nostril, jaw, tongue and eyeball movements as well as nasal secretions and penile changes! Some behaviour! More simply, flehmen consists of curling the upper lip upward, wrinkling the nose and baring the gum. The head and neck are extended upwards, the lower jaw may be rhythmically lowered and raised, the teeth may be parted slightly, and the tongue arched against the palate. The lower lip may droop and quiver. The eyes roll downward, and the head may be rotated slowly from side to side. The penis may be partially or completely protruded. During and following the flehmen response a small amount of clear fluid usually drips from each nostril. The behaviour is much more common in stallions than in mares and usually follows prolonged sniffing of urine. It is thought to be involved in the analysis of odours in urine, and aids in the detection of mares in oestrus. The behaviour probably facilitates the movement of material into the vomeronasal organ, which is an accessory olfactory organ.

In summary, whenever I see signs of sex I assume that the horse is sexually motivated to some extent and that this motivation will interfere with performance. I note this in my race book simply as **Sex signs**, followed by a brief description. I write **Visible vulva** if a filly or mare has raised or displaced her tail so that I can see her perineum, or **Dangling dick** if a colt, horse or gelding is protruding his penis. If a filly or mare is swishing her tail and spurting urine I write **On heat** and rule them out of contention straight away. If I see a horse masturbating I record **Big swinging dick** in my race book. I am pleased to report that I have been able to make this entry on one memorable occasion. And finally, if I see a horse laugh, I write down **Flehmen**.

Chapter 9 Mounting yard misbehaviour

The strapper

The first thing I look at when a horse enters the mounting yard is not the horse, of course, but the strapper. And the first thing I do is to count the number of strappers. Every now and then a horse turns up in the yard without a strapper and is led by the clerk of the course. Maybe the trainer has had a heart attack in the birdcage and the strapper is required for cardiopulmonary resuscitation? Maybe it's a one trainer, no strapper, outfit, and the trainer is lying dead in the stall? As you can see, I usually fear the worst. I don't have a category or variable for this occasional, perhaps dreadful, occurrence. I simply cross the horse out in my race book.

Having established that there is at least one strapper I then make sure that I haven't got double vision and that there aren't **Two strappers**. This also fills me with foreboding. If a horse requires two strappers to control it, how bad is it? My mind immediately goes racing back to Oscar Schindler, the magnificent beast that required three strappers to restrain him before the 96 Cup. He still sometimes bobs up at nights to swish his tail in my face. Oh, dear. What a nightmare! At carnival time you will often notice that the trainer of a foreign invader will accompany the horse and strapper as they walk from birdcage to mounting yard. That's cool, if he's just having a pleasant stroll in the Australian sun with his horse. But if he's holding a second leading strap or has his hand on rein or bridle, I immediately fear the worst (Photo 30). Two strappers used to be a rare occurrence, but is increasing in popularity. For example, Myles Plumb, the personal trainer for Lloyd Williams, generally uses two strappers. Because of its increasing prominence I have upgraded two strappers to the status of a proper variable in my race book.

Photo 30
Easy Virtue, Two strappers,
Flemington, 8 November 2001.

The next task is to establish whether the strapper is moving. A stationary strapper generally means that the horse has baulked, and I note it regardless of whether it is a minor hesitation, where the horse has momentarily come to a complete halt, or a full-blown refusal to move forward. **Baulking** (Photo 31) is a much more common and less intense form of shying, which I will discuss later (*see* page 135). Baulkers can assume a stubborn, immobile state and fight against all attempts to move them on. Andrew Fraser, a Canadian ethologist, has described how confirmed baulkers can often remain in this state for hours, if they are left alone. They can often be made to move by moving them backwards, promptly. However, bad baulkers may be so bad that no management technique is successful. The best recent example from the racetrack is the five-year-old mare Pravda, in the 2000 Melbourne Cup. Pravda propped in the middle of the straight and refused to proceed to the barrier, despite the attention of two attendants, two mounted clerks of the course and the jockey. Andrew notes that cruel force cannot be justified in attempts to make such horses move. It is known to be ineffective anyway. Fortunately for Pravda the clerks are superb horsemen and knew this too. And, fortunately for the backers of Pravda, she was scratched from the race. Why did she baulk? There are several possible causes of baulking, including temperament and pain. In some cases the horse may sense a task which it cannot perform. You need to be part of the hullabaloo at Flemington on Cup Day to fully appreciate the task ahead of Pravda. There is a cacophony of sound. A pulsating wall of noise. I have no doubt that Pravda slammed right into it.

Photo 31
Richland, Baulking,
Flemington, 12 May 2001.

Having finally established that there is but a single, non-stationary strapper, I can get down to business. I have already described in Chapter 6 some of the remarkable effects of human contact on horse behaviour, so it will come as no surprise for you to find that I need another seven variables to define the relationship between strapper and horse in the mounting yard. It is of course easy to detect boisterous or fractious behaviour by watching the horse, but watching the strapper is equally productive. I record **Tugging**, **Sloping strapper**, **Two hands**, **Shoulder**, **Circling**, **Positive strapper** and **Strapper remarks**. All these variables indicate the extent to which the horse is under control.

Tugging on the strap is often observed if the horse baulks or is showing poor head behaviour. More on this shortly. Sometimes you need to be a little bit careful with tugging to distinguish it from a regular pull on the strap used by some strappers to keep their horses focused. Rhythmic jigging or pulling can often have a calming effect. I regard tugging as a violent pull on the strap, generally in response to bad behaviour. It is often accompanied by strapper anger or frustration and a comment such as "What's wrong with ya, hey?" Tugging can have undesirable effects on the horse's mouth, and cause bruising of the lips, tongue or bars, especially if the bit is poorly adjusted.

Once in a blue moon you will see a strapper violently hit a horse. I am not referring to mild rebukes, but to forceful hits, slaps or punches to the face, head or neck. I would advise horse watchers to show restraint in this situation and not leap over the mounting yard fence and remonstrate with the strapper. Violence by or towards strappers is not condoned. Simply record **Negative strapper** in your race book. If you happen to be the owner of the horse concerned I would seek out a new trainer. Punishment is probably the least effective method of training both horses and humans. If it is to be effective the punishment must be associated with the undesired behaviour and not the handler. Thus if a strapper hits a horse for misbehaviour it may become more fearful of the handler, which exacerbates the original fearful behaviour, and provokes the use of more severe punishment in the management of the horse. This is a vicious circle which can lead to physical abuse of the horse.

Sloping strapper (Photo 32) is probably my favourite variable. Generally the horse is moving at a fast gait and the strapper is having trouble restraining it. He or she leans backwards at an angle, digging in his or her heels. If the strapper was sloping at a forwards angle, it would generally mean that the horse has bolted and the strapper was hanging on for dear life. Another way to think of sloping strapper is that it is the horse that is leading the strapper. Or simply, the horse is

Photo 32
Grey Regent, Sloping strapper,
Flemington, 16 December 2000.

Photo 33
Armorda, Two hands, Salivating,
Flemington, 12 March 2001.

pulling. **Two hands** (Photo 33) is self-explanatory in that the strapper simply uses two hands to control the horse. One hand holding the leading strap, the other either pushing on the horse's shoulder, head or neck, or holding onto the off-side rein. Two hands can be a bit tricky, and is probably the reason I missed backing Brew in the 2000 Melbourne Cup. Brew was perfect, but the strapper was using two hands as he went past my spot. I realised later that I was standing on the corner of the mounting yard, and it is quite OK to use two hands to direct a horse around a corner.

Photo 34
Reactive, Shoulder,
Flemington, 16 March 2002.

Shoulder (Photo 34) is similar to two hands in that it indicates how much effort the strapper needs to put in to direct the horse. The strapper simply leans into the horse, pushing his/her shoulder into the shoulder region of the horse. **Circling** (Photo 35) is often seen with

Photo 35
Number 11, Loong Har, Circling out of the parade,
Moonee Valley, 9 December 2000.

Photo 36
Fayrouz, Positive strapper,
Moonee Valley, 5 May 2001.

baulking horses or horses that need too much shoulder or two hands. The strapper breaks the horse out of the parade and circles it on the mounting yard grass. Positive strapper is the same as the variable I record in the birdcage. If the strapper is touching or petting the horse in any way with his/her free hand I write **Positive strapper** (Photo 36) in my race book. The strapper is using two hands, but in a very different way! And as before in the birdcage, I give bonus marks for strappers stroking the withers region of the horse and write **Very positive strapper**.

As I'm assessing the relationship between strapper and horse I pay attention to whatever the strapper may be saying. It may be sweet nothings, murmured with affection into the horse's ear, in which case I would note **Positive strapper**. Or it may be simple instructions in plain English, which the horse is meant to understand and willingly obey. Or it may be loud and profane verbal abuse. These comments often give me a clear understanding of the relationship between strapper and horse and the horse's temperament and current mental attitude. I started writing down these remarks in my race book, and eventually realised that I was scoring another variable. So, **Strapper remarks** is now a fully-fledged variable, complete with a Top Twenty and a strapper's prize.

The Top Twenty, in no particular order, are:

1. "He hasn't travelled in the greatest"
2. "Don't"
3. "Don't do that shit"
4. "No, no, ... I said no"
5. "Just walk"
6. "Settle...., settle...., fucking settle"
7. "Watch it mate, this one kicks"
8. "I've got this dog"
9. "Jesus, you're a bitch"
10. "You fucking crazy bastard"
11. "What's got into you?"

12. "Wake up to yourself"
13. "Not today, Roy"
14. "I've got a pushy one"
15. "Behave!"
16. "Cut it out, you cunt"
17. "Take it easy"
18. "He's got a bee in his bum" - uttered in response to a horse shaking itself like a wet dog
19. "He's too hot"
20. "Stupid, stupid".

And the strapper's prize goes to ...."I don't get paid enough for this".

I often hear positive remarks, such as "Put 20 on it for me", or "He feels so strong", or "This one will win, mate", but I treat comments such as these as neutral remarks since, although they are ostensibly positive, long experience suggests otherwise.

One last thing about strappers. Although I'm very cool about most human vices, especially drinking, gambling and vacuum cleaning in the nude, I'm most uncool about smoking. If secondary smoke is deemed to be harmful to humans, then I imagine it is also harmful to horses. I put a black mark in my race book if I see a **Strapper smoking**. Strappers should also be advised that smoking stunts your growth. If you are not careful you could end up as a jockey.

Gait

The mounting yard is an excellent spot to check out a horse's gait. The trouble is, the best surface on which to watch a horse walking is bitumen. And it took me a long time to realise that it is not the watching that is so important, but the listening. You can hear the sounds of the feet as they land - clip, clop, clip, clop, clip, clop. In Melbourne, Caulfield is the best track for listening because there is bitumen all the way from the birdcage, through the parade ring, and up to the mounting yard. Unfortunately for horse listeners, the mounting yard, like all other metropolitan mounting yards, has those red rubberised bricks, which cushion the sound of the footfall, and make it harder to evaluate the gait. But by tuning in your ear to the rhythm of the gait you can still easily evaluate whether it is normal, fast or slow. Clip....Clop....Clip....Clop is the gait of a **Slow** horse. ClipClopClipClopClipClop is the gait of a **Fast** horse. Moonee Valley seems to be replacing its old hard bitumen with new rubberised stuff, which muffles the sound of the footfall. However, if the strapper is striding or jogging it is a sure sign that the horse has a fast gait.

I remember one day at Caulfield when Gary Fennesy, stable foreman for the late Peter Hayes, was on his mobile, presumably talking to the boss: "He's walking about half an inch at a time. They're all banked up behind him!" He was describing Civil List, the number 1 saddlecloth, walking up the laneway to the mounting yard, slowing up the traffic. Civil List finished fourth of nine runners in a 1400 metre race at 5/1. I always assume that slow horses like Civil List are not aroused enough to win, and that fast horses are over-aroused, and more likely to lose.

There are four main types of gait in the horse. The walk is an even four-beat gait, with two feet in contact with the ground at any one time. The trot is a two-beat gait where the foreleg on one side moves in unison with the hind leg on the other. The canter is a three beat gait in which two of the diagonal legs are paired and the other foreleg and hind leg act independently. The gallop is a four-beat gait, with a period when all four feet are off the ground. Stephen Budiansky gives a good account of the mechanics of horse movement in *The Nature of Horses*, but for the most part this need not concern horse watchers. In the mounting yard you will only see the walk and the trot. If a horse is changing gait, between the walk and trot, I mark in my race book **Changing gait**. This is a very bad sign, and indicates that the horse is unsettled or aroused. An extreme change of gait occurs when a horse starts rearing, bucking, or pigrooting. The horse may suddenly rear up, as in shying, or plant the forelegs stiffly on the ground and kick up with the hind legs. Racegoers who have attended a rodeo will be familiar with these behaviour patterns. Horses that perform any of these behaviours are marked in my book as **Bucking** (Photo 37). I assume that they are over-aroused and unlikely to perform at their optimum. And that is a mild understatement.

Photo 37
Unbridled Secret, Bucking,
Caulfield, 1 April 2002.

While looking at the horse's gait you should also check out its action, which is a term used to describe the amount of flexion of the knees and hocks. Racehorses have, or should have a free-moving, long-striding, "daisy-cutting" action. In contrast, the highly trained Lippizaner stallions at the Spanish Riding School in Vienna have a very high knee and hock action. I describe a horse that trots with a very high action as **Prancing** (*see* Photo 27). Prancing is usually accompanied by a pronounced arched neck, with the horse pivoting its head downward from the poll, and often to one side. Most punters would describe a prancing horse as being **"On the toe"**. In itself, prancing is probably not a fault, unless the horse is changing gait constantly from walk to prance and back to walk. Some punters like horses to be "on the toe", but have trouble distinguishing them from horses that are **Changing gait**. The easiest method is to check for other signs of fractious behaviour. If the horse shows poor head behaviour it is more likely to be changing gait than prancing. If the horse has its head under control and an arched neck then it is more likely to be prancing.

Finally, I check out the horse's stride. In a normal stride, the same side hind foot should strike the ground more or less on top of the footprint of the forefoot. The American horseplayer and handicapper, Joe Takach, makes a big deal of "walking short". Joe reckons that the hind feet need to clear the hoof prints of the front feet for the horse to be walking well. I'm much less fussy and I record **Short stride** in my race book only if the hind foot lands greater than one horseshoe length behind the imprint of the forefoot. There may be many reasons for a short stride. The horse may be tired, or injured, or in pain, or the strapper may have a strong hold that prevents the horse walking freely, or it may even be a normal short strider. For the moment, it's probably best to keep an open mind on whether it's a useful indicator of performance until I reveal some statistics in Chapter 11.

If a horse oversteps you might occasionally here a "clicking" or "clacking" sound, which is the result of the hind and front shoes striking together. This is a gait defect generally known as forging. It could be the result of a shoeing problem, a conformation problem, or an injury. I make a note of it for future reference, although I use the term **Clacking** because of its wonderful onomatopoeia. I also make a note if I see a horse stumbling.

If you look for long enough at walking horses you will start to see some funny legs and some very abnormal gaits. There are bow-legged horses, pigeon-toed horses, calf-kneed, cow-hocked, camped under and camped out horses (Figure 9.1).

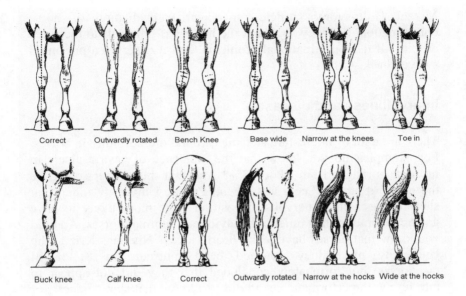

Figure 9.1
Some conformational faults in the fore and hind limbs of horses.
Reprinted from M. Holmström, The effects of conformation, in Equine
Locomotion, edited by W. Back and H.M. Clayton, 2001, pp. 281-295,
by permission of the publisher W.B. Saunders.

There are even technical terms for some of these faults, such as
dishing when the horse flicks out a foreleg, or plaiting, when its feet
get in the way of one another and it looks like it might fall over. I
don't worry too much about all these faults since they are
conformational rather than behavioural problems. But a lot of people
do place a lot of store by conformation. I'm afraid I'm not one of
them. If you are interested, you should probably ditch this book and
pick up Nick Mordin's *The Winning Look*. Nick is a pommy punter
and reckons that he has yet to see a decent horse with a dipped back,
and that horses with squashed short necks are usually slow! If you
are still seriously interested, a good place to start reading could be

Mikael Holmström's article on objective evaluation of horse conformation. My view is that if the horse has got itself to the races despite all its conformational problems then it deserves a pat on its swayed back.

Injury, illness and disease

There are a lot of interesting statistics around on morbidity in horses. For example, did you know that the incidence of gastric ulcers in racehorses ranges from 81 to 93%? And that these ulcers could be the result of stress? Scott McClure at Purdue University found that show horses with a nervous disposition were more likely to have gastric ulceration than quiet or behaviourally normal horses. And did you know that horses have leaky heart valves? Nikolaus Kriz at the University of Sydney detected heart murmurs in 81.1% of racehorses, but fortunately concluded that they did not appear to interfere with performance. And did you know that shin soreness, or dorsal metacarpal disease, affects 42-80% of two-year-olds in their first year of training? When you consider these statistics, it's a wonder we have horse races at all.

The most important injuries and disease affecting the racehorse are lameness and respiratory disease. C.J. Bailey from the University of Sydney followed the fate of a group of 169 horses from the Sydney Easter yearling sale of 1995. An astounding 85% suffered at least one incident of injury or disease while they were in training. Shin soreness was the most common condition in two-year-olds (42%), followed by fetlock problems (25%) and coughs and nasal discharge (16%). And 13% suffered from lacerations or traumatic injuries.

My general attitude to illness and injury when I first started watching horses was that it was too hard to detect and that I could safely leave it to the experts - the trainer and the veterinary stewards. However, I then read about a fascinating trial conducted by the Western Australian Turf Club. All two-year-old horses were examined by the vets. If a horse showed a pain response to touching of the shin (i.e.

withdrawal of the leg) it was scratched from the day's race and not permitted to race for six weeks. J.B. Griffiths has published an analysis of the effect of this program. Horses appeared to race in a more predictable manner, with a significant reduction in the number of lengths between first and last after the program was initiated. It seems that the program deterred trainers from presenting horses to race with shin soreness. This doesn't really help horse watchers much in trying to detect lameness. You really need to be able to touch the horse to see if it is tender. But it does confirm that sore horses are going around each week.

Lameness is probably the hardest thing to detect and takes years of experience. Even the experts can get it wrong. The furore over whether Universal Prince was lame or fit to start in the 2001 Cup is an example. Bede Murray was adamant that the horse was OK, the veterinary stewards were equally adamant that the horse was lame. I do not know which expert was right, but I find it reassuring to know that one has to be wrong. I also know that apparently lame horses can make fools of us all - trainers, vets and horse watchers alike.

Doug Butler has described some of the approaches to detecting lameness. The most straightforward is probably simple observation of the horse in motion, walking or trotting towards and away from you. With lameness in a foreleg the horse will appear to favour the lame leg by dropping more heavily on the sound one. If you watch the level of the horse's poll and it rises and falls with each step then this is a good sign of lameness. The lame leg is the one that hits the ground as the head bobs up. Lameness originating from a shoulder often shows up as short stepping on the affected side and dragging the toe. Hind leg lameness is best detected by looking at the croup instead of the head and looking for a dip in the hip on one side. The lame leg is on the opposite side to the dipping, in other words, the hip will bob up (hip hike) when the lame leg bears weight. However, the causes of lameness are complex and a simple technique such as looking for head bobs and hip hikes is not infallible. And even if you can detect lameness with confidence, you are unlikely to see it very often. Noah Cohen, from Texas A&M University, reported on a study of 43,865 race starts by thoroughbreds in Kentucky. One hundred and ninety-two horses were injured, which equates to an injury rate of 4.4 per 1000 race starts, or about one horse every two race meetings.

Detection of respiratory disease is much easier. I simply make a note if a horse coughs or has a runny nose. **Coughing** and **Nasal discharge** are pretty good indicators of inflammatory changes in the airways which are likely to lead to reduced performance. I'll also make a note if I see signs of recent traumatic injury, such as a bruise, laceration or wound. Fortunately, I don't get to make these notes in my race book very often.

Language

"If only they could talk". I wouldn't mind a dollar for every time I've heard that at the racetrack. But of course, horses can talk. The most famous talking horse was Mister Ed, the palomino star of the sixties TV show. According to Alan Young, the actor who played Wilbur Post, the method used by Ed's trainer Lester Hilton to make him talk was "a little like having peanut butter stuck under your top lip and then trying to get rid of it". This seems unlikely since it would be hard to manipulate the peanut butter to cue Ed to start and stop talking. A more likely explanation is that Lester made him talk by placing a wire in his mouth. Tugging on the wire caused him to move his lips. In fact, there is one photograph in Alan Young's book which shows Ed and Lester on the set (*Mister Ed and Me*, page 28). If you look carefully you can just make out the wire held in Lester's hand. I hope this hasn't spoilt any of the magic for the little kiddies out there, but now they are grown up baby-boomers, I'm sure they can cope. The interesting thing is that horses don't need peanut butter or a wire in their mouth to express their feelings. They are capable of communicating a wide range of emotions using the equipment they have to hand, especially the **Head**, the **Ears** and the **Tail**.

The expert on horse talk is Marthe Kiley-Worthington, of the University of Exeter in the UK. Marthe has done detailed studies of both vocal and visual communication in horses. Horses make two non-vocal sounds using the respiratory tract - the sigh and the snort, and they make three basic sounds using the larynx or vocal chords - the nicker, whinny, and squeal. And of course, they also sneeze.

The **Sigh** seems to occur in horses in much the same situations as in humans, when there is a change in activity related to boredom. Thus a horse may sigh when being saddled up and about to be taken out and ridden. The meaning seems to be "Oh, no, here we go again".

The **Snort** is a more demonstrative call. It is uttered by exhaling rapidly through the nostrils so that they vibrate, and lasts for about 0.5 seconds. Snorts can be quite loud, and according to Marthe can be heard from a distance of 200 metres. I know I'm nearly deaf in my left ear and the racetrack is noisy, but I reckon maybe 20 metres, 50 metres maximum. I'd certainly recommend that you take up a position handy to the mounting yard fence to hear them. The snort appears to be an alarm call and is given in potentially fearful situations. For example, the startle response of a horse to a frightening stimulus may consist of a jump, followed by orientation towards the stimulus, then freezing for 20 seconds or so, followed by a loud snort. Alternatively, the animal may flee, stop, orientate, and snort. The meaning seems to be "There is danger here". Snorts may also be a way of attracting attention and can be heard in both playful situations and when a horse is excited. The meaning seems to be "I am here".

The **Nicker** is a soft call given with the mouth shut but the nostrils extended. It is a low-pitched call uttered in a series of pulses. It is common when there is a greeting between mare and foal, handler and horse, stallion and oestrus mare, and stable mates. It can be heard up to 30 metres. The meaning seems to be "G'day, mate".

The **Whinny** or neigh is the most characteristic call of the horse. It is a loud call, up to 2.8 seconds long, given with the mouth open and generally of a high pitch. It is most often heard when horses are separated and has been most commonly described as a distress call. However, since the call can be heard up to 800 metres away, and since it is usually answered, it is more likely that it is a distance contact call. Horses that are whinnying generally show more locomotion than horses that are nickering, and this is probably a reflection of their greater arousal. Whinnying is also heard when a stallion approaches an oestrus mare, and I'm pretty sure that in this context the stallion is saying "Look at me, I'm here". So, the meaning seems to be "Hey, here I am" rather than "Help".

The **Squeal** is a loud call that starts with the mouth shut, but then opens so that the corners of the mouth are drawn back. The pitch of the call may rise so that in some horses it sounds more like a scream. It last between 0.3 and 1 second, and is often repeated, and can be heard up to 100 metres. Often the ears may be laid back. The squeal is given in several situations, especially as a defensive greeting. It is heard in free-ranging horses when they are forming a dominance hierarchy and many bites are being exchanged. A squeal may also be a response to pain. So, the meaning seems to be "Stop. Don't push me".

When tape recordings of nickers, whinnies, squeals and snorts are played back to horses they respond to nickers and whinnies, but not to snorts and squeals. This makes sense if you remember that whinnies and nickers function primarily as contact calls, whereas snorts and squeals reflect alarm and fear.

In summary, horses are primarily visual communicators, and have only a small repertoire of sounds that are infrequently used. At the racetrack I make a note of whinnies, squeals and snorts in my race book, whenever I hear them. I don't bother recording nickers and sighs since they are low arousal sounds. Squealing is too rare to be a useful variable (but *see* Ebony Grosve, Chapter 14, page 211),

Whinnying is uncommon (but *see* Lochrae, Chapter 4, page 59) and **Snorting** is reasonably common. I assume that if I hear a horse vocalisation then the horse is aroused to some extent, and this arousal may detract from its race performance.

Posture

Horses have a much larger repertoire of visual signals. The general posture of a horse, in particular the position of its head, is a good indicator of the level of excitement or arousal. In general, and in common with most other animals, the higher the position of the head, the greater the level of arousal. The lower the position of the head, the lower the level of arousal. At the two extremes, a horse with its head down and eyes half closed could be going to sleep, a horse with its head up could be rearing and going berserk. In between these extremes is probably the optimum head position for a racehorse. Alert. The head is held at an angle of about 45° to the vertical. If a horse holds its head below this alert posture I'm not fussed. It means that it's relaxed, if not sleepy. If a horse holds its head above this position, I become very concerned and write in my race book **Head up** (Photo 38).

The head is also extremely important because it carries all the sense organs, and in order to bring these organs to bear on a stimulus the horse generally has to move its head. This is called orientation. But because a horse's eyes are on the side of its head and because they are brown and black it is difficult to see where a horse is looking by watching the eyes. But it is commonly observed that when a horse looks at something in the distance it raises its head and lifts its nose and when a horse looks at much closer objects it may arch the neck and rotate the head to one side. Researchers in the Department of Psychology at the University of Western Australia, led by Alison Harman, have made a detailed study of the eye of the horse in order to understand this head moving behaviour. They found that the horse can see a very narrow but panoramic view quite clearly. Visual acuity above and below this narrow horizontal strip is poor. This area

Photo 38
The Mooksta, Head up and Ears side,
Flemington, 16 December 2000.

of vision is perceived by a region in the retina with a very high concentration of light sensitive cells - called the visual streak.

Tests of the horse's visual field show that the binocular field, where the vision from both eyes overlaps, is about 80°. Alison Harman reckons that the horse has a quite a large blind spot straight in front of its forehead, and has to raise its nose considerably to see directly in front. Alison also believes that this blind spot in front of the horse is about the width of the horse. When the horse is ridden "on the bit", with its nose just in front of a vertical position, it cannot see anything directly in front of it and must rely on the jockey. When the horse is looking at something close, such as a lump of sugar in the hand, the horse arches it neck and rotates its head in order to utilise binocular vision down the nose. Alison thinks that horses probably don't pay attention to their front and lateral visual fields at the same time. When the horse is distracted by something in its peripheral vision it will turn its head or whole body towards the object and raise its head to use its binocular vision.

Photo 39
Eliza Park, Head in,
Sandown, 7 April 2001.

I always assume that if a horse is alert as it is being led by the strapper around the mounting yard and its head is pointing straight ahead then it is looking ahead and concentrating. If it is looking to either side with both eyes, then it may not be concentrating. So, I note orientation of the head in my race book as **Head in** (Photo 39), if the horse has turned or rotated its head to the nearside, towards the strapper, or **Head out** (Photo 40), if the horse has turned or rotated its head toward the offside, or away from the strapper. Head out is probably a better indicator of whether the horse is distracted by extraneous stimuli, such as the racetrack crowd, noise or other parading horses. A head in horse could be simply attending to strapper stimuli, but unless I see positive behaviour from the strapper, I cannot be sure of this. If a horse has its head in or head out, and is showing head up behaviour as well, I regard it as a very poor conveyance. In fact head up and head out can develop into **Shying**. This is the most extreme form of head up behaviour and probably one of the most sensational sights that can be seen in the mounting yard. A horse will suddenly rear up on its hind legs, and turn sharply away to one side. It may even start squealing and

Photo 40
Heart's Hope, Head out,
Sandown, 6 March 2002.

trembling. Shying is essentially an intense alarm reaction. The horse is fearful. Or simply, it is spooked. The main feature of shying is the sudden elevation of the head, neck, forelimbs or the whole body. Shying horses are apparently responding to visual stimuli such as reflected light, fluttering pieces of paper or cloth, or even the sudden movement of small pesky animals in their immediate vicinity. Strange and sudden loud noises can also elicit the response. For a horse that is really spooked, shying can often be followed by **Bolting**. Fortunately, bolters are generally scratched from the race, saving punters much anguish!

A particular form of head up behaviour that deserves special attention is **Head tossing**. The horse repeatedly tosses its head from a relaxed normal or down position to head up. A similar behaviour is

Head shaking, where the movement is from side to side rather than up and down. Head tossing may be an initial response to some sort of irritation, or a problem with the bit, or a problem with the rider. But the behaviour then persists as a bad habit. I don't like the behaviour when I see it in a strange horse and would score it as head up. But if I have seen the horse several times and I know it is a confirmed tosser, then I can sometimes pretend not to notice if the horse has no other faults. Head shaking is also a common response to irritation, especially by insects, around the head and ears. Localized quivering of the skin or **Skin twitching** can also be a response to skin irritation, and occurs mainly along the shoulder and forearm. It mostly seems to be induced by biting insects attempting to land on or stay on the skin.

Robert Cook, a US veterinarian and expert on head shaking, has pointed out how placing a foreign object, the bit, into the mouth of a horse, sets up a train of sensory responses which signal the brain to think "Eat". Accordingly, motor responses initiate lip movement, tongue movement, salivation and chewing. At the same time responses from the legs and lungs signal the brain to think "Exercise". Physiologically, we are asking the horse to eat and exercise simultaneously. These two functions are mutually exclusive and incompatible, so the horse gets confused. And one of the signs of confusion and frustration is head shaking. Robert asks the question: "How would we feel if we were required to run around the garden with a bunch of keys in our mouth?" I've been thinking carefully about this and I reckon that I would probably baulk, and then toss or shake my head.

After a horse has orientated its head the ears will orientate on the object. The **Ears** are probably the best indicator of a horse's emotions. I regard them as the window to a horse's soul. And the best thing about them is that they are easy to see, sitting pretty on top of the head. Horses generally point their ears in the same direction as they are looking. In the alert horse they are pricked and facing forwards (*see* Photo 17), and the horse is looking straight ahead. If the ears are turned to the **Side** (Photo 41) or slightly back, the horse is generally looking to the side, and could be described as disinterested. The most dramatic ear position is when they are laid **Back** (*see* Photo 24) and rotated onto the side of the head. This ear position is associated with aggressive and defensive horses, and could easily be followed up with a bite or a kick.

Photo 41
Gallopini, Ears side,
Caulfield, 17 February 2001.

Each ear of the horse has 13 sets of muscles controlling its movement so that they are capable of amazing independent movement. If a stimulus is not sufficiently interesting for a horse to orientate towards by turning its head it can simply swivel one or both ears. The ears can often be constantly on the move, scanning the environment for interesting, diverting, threatening or distracting stimuli. I regard a lot of ear movement as a bad sign in a racehorse, and an indicator that it is not totally focused on the task ahead. In particular, if I notice a horse constantly flicking it ears from pricked to backwards, then I will record **Ear flicking** in my race book (*see* Photo 20). There is no published research on ear movement, but Ocean Hartrick, a psychology student at Massey University, has done an interesting pilot study. She asked 40 vet students, with various levels of confidence and experience with horses, to lead a horse around a simple obstacle course. Ocean measured ear movement and position, resistance from the horse and some human behaviour variables. Confidence and attitude of the students was measured with a questionnaire. She found a very significant correlation between ear movement and human attitude. In other words, the more positive the attitude of the student towards horses, the less the horse's ears moved. This suggests that people who like horses will have a positive effect on them, and that people that are uncertain about horses may communicate this uncertainty to the horse. Ocean's work certainly confirms my view that ear flicking may indicate uncertain horses.

After the ears I know I should look at the horse's nostrils and lips, but I must confess, I generally don't. I have no real excuse apart from being overworked at the racetrack. But since there are 10 sets of muscles serving the nose, lips and mouth, and the horse's face is capable of great variation in expression, I thought I'd better check with the expert. I flashed off an email to Marthe Kiley-Worthington to ask her if I should be watching out for flared nostrils in racehorses. And of course, Marthe confirmed that I should. Flaring of the nostrils seems to be connected with excitement, and regardless of whether the cause is fear, aggression, frustration or pleasure, it is an indicator of arousal. So, overworked that I am, I have now started recording **Flared nostrils** in my race book. The best example I have seen is one of the Parthenon sculptures in the British Museum (Photo 42). The simple description below the head of the horse sums it up:

> The head of a horse from the chariot of the moon-goddess, Selene. The horse is weary from its night long labour: the eye bulges, the nostrils flare, and the mouth gapes.

Now there's some understatement. How can a broken fragment of marble nearly 2500 years old be so expressive? Is it because the head is protruding over the pediment? Is it because you can make out the veins and sense the tautness of the skin? Is it the excellence of the flared nostrils?

Photo 42
Unknown horse, Flared nostrils and Gaping,
Parthenon, 438 BC.

Like the head, the tail can be very important in communication too. In fact, when one goes up, the other often does too. Like the head, increasing elevation of the tail is associated with increasing excitement or arousal. But to fully appreciate the tail of a horse you need to examine a skeleton. I'm not sure where the best place to do this is nowadays. When I was a lad they had a terrific display on the evolution of the horse in the Melbourne Museum, from little *Eohippuses* up to the modern day *Equus*. You could have a good squiz at horse skeletons. The spine of a horse is composed of 54 vertebrae. The coccygeal or tail region has on average 18 vertebrae, which leads to the amazing statistic that a horse's tail makes up one third of its spine! Of course, the vertebrae are getting smaller as you approach the tip, but even so, some tail! And it makes a wonderful fly whisk.

Photo 43
Unknown horse, Relaxed tail,
Moonee Valley, 24 March 2001.

When you look at a horse's tail you tend to forget that underneath all that beautiful hair is a very flexible skeleton. When the tail is relaxed it hangs straight down behind the horse and swishes ever so gently from side to side as the horse walks (Photo 43). The coccygeal vertebrae are probably dangling at an angle of somewhere between 0 and 10° from the vertical. As the horse becomes aroused the tail stiffens and projects outwards at an angle of anywhere between 20 and 90° from the vertical. In other words, it can stick straight out. And an excited horse can raise the tail above the level of the back line. On top of variation in the elevation of the tail it can show varying amounts of lateral or sideways movements. This is variously described as swishing, flicking, switching, wagging, flaring or flagging. And on top of all this the tail is invariably raised to urinate and defaecate, and actively pressed flat if the horse is frightened from behind.

Photo 44
Magic Chance, Stiff tail,
Moonee Valley, 24 March 2001.

So, what is the horse watcher to record? I simply note if the tail is not relaxed. I mark in my race book **Stiff** (Photo 44) if the tail is elevated to any extent. I am very careful if I see a horse flicking or swishing its tail (Photo 45). I ask myself, is it the fly season? And is the horse simply flicking at flies? If the tail returns to the relaxed position the answer is generally yes, and I would regard the tail as relaxed. If there are no flies and the tail remains stiff, I would record **Stiff/swished** in my book. Actually, I'm glad I'm not a fly. I've been swished a couple of times when hanging over the mounting yard rail, and it gives you a real hurry-up. In dressage events horses that swish their tails are marked down for showing signs of resistance. A horse can also swish its tail as a threatening response to another horse. And

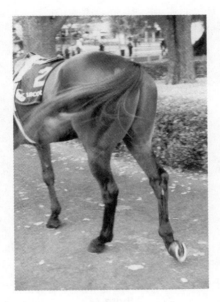

Photo 45
Unknown horse, Swished tail,
Moonee Valley, 5 May 2001.

of course humans soon learn to stand clear if a horse swishes its tail as it is often followed by a kick.

Recently I have also started recording if the tail is pressed **Flat**, **Plaited** (Photo 46) or shows signs of wear. I don't know if these are good or bad signs, but I'm suspicious of plaited tails as they imply that the horse is a show pony and a lot of time has been devoted to its appearance and I'm suspicious of signs of wear as it implies that the horse may have a **Tail-rubbing** problem in the home stable.

Once they've jumped and are racing a horse often shows resentment of jockey vigour or use of the whip by switching its tail. Jennifer Weeks and Alan Beck at Purdue University did an interesting little study of tail swishing in horses. Seventeen horses, both mares and

Photo 46
Unknown horse, Plaited tail,
Flemington, 12 May 2001.

geldings, were ridden by riders with three different levels of experience - beginner, intermediate and advanced. They found a much greater increase in tail swishing with beginning riders than with intermediate or advanced riders. It seems that agitation in the horses, as indicated by tail swishing, was linked to the inexperience of the beginning riders. This inexperience may make the rider less sensitive to the way they treat the horse.

Prior to urination and defaecation the tail is elevated and flared in a characteristic attitude. I record this in my race book as **Flared tail** (Photo 47). With practice you will notice a clear difference in the appearance of a flared and a stiff/swished tail. If the horse proceeds to **Urinate** (Photo 48) and it is a filly or mare I would record this in

Photo 47
Varsilayos, Flared tail,
Moonee Valley, 24 March 2001.

my race book as a **Sex sign**. Horses can defaecate while moving with the tail lifted, but nearly always urinate standing still. They can be trained to urinate in a stable or box by freeing them from restraint, forking up the straw bedding, and whistling a long vibrating-type note. If a male horse was urinating in the mounting yard, then it could only be Subzero putting on a show, since he is the only male I have observed urinating there in the last five years of watching. If the horse proceeds to defaecate I write **Dumping** (Photo 49) in my book.

George Waring in his book *Horse Behavior* provides some fascinating statistics on elimination. The daily faecal output of a horse is in the range 14-23 kg. That is quite a pile! And the normal daily urine volume ranges from 3-18 ml per kilogram of body weight. An adult thoroughbred weighing say 440 kg might have a daily urine output of nearly 8 litres. That is some pissing! Clearly, the chances of observing elimination behaviour at the racetrack are quite high.

Photo 48
Unknown horse, Urinating,
Sandown, 7 April 2001.

Photo 49
Magneto, Dumping,
Flemington, 12 May 2001.

Feral and free-ranging horses spend a lot of time investigating and smelling dung piles before adding to the heap themselves. In the mounting yard the strapper will of course restrain a horse from attempting to smell a dung pile, but you may notice that one heap of dung tends to stimulate other horses to dump at that spot.

Horses can often flare their tails as if to dump, but then fail to deliver the goods. I don't record the number, amount or consistency of the dump, but I am considering it. Rat psychologists spend most of their lives watching rats in an open field, which is a kind of mounting yard for rats, and counting the number of faecal boli, which is a polite word for rat dirt. The number of dumps and the rate of dumping are used as a measure of emotionality, or nervousness, in the rat. If it's good enough for rat psychologists, then it should be good enough for horse watchers.

Chapter 10 They're on the track!

As the horses leave the mounting yard and head out onto the track I have a good look to see if any are **Sweating**. This must be one of the most misunderstood signs of poor performance in a racehorse. As we found in the looksee study, sweating on its own was totally unreliable as an indicator of potential losers. Most casual horse watchers are convinced that a horse which sweats up will perform poorly. This is despite ample evidence to the contrary. I always remember Stedamink! It might be over 20 years since the 1981 Spring Carnival, but the mare Stedamink left an indelible impression on me and all at Flemington who saw her leave the mounting yard in an absolute muck lather. She romped in at 25/1. Her trainer remarked laconically after the race: "She always sweats up".

Horses, like humans, will sweat for two reasons; because they are hot and because they are nervous. Let's deal with hot horses first. The Australian experts on hot horses are David Hodgson and Finola McConaghy in the Department of Animal Health at the University of Sydney. They have written an excellent review of thermoregulation in the horse. The horse has an amazing ability to increase its metabolic rate some 90 times in response to the energy requirements of exercise. But the process of converting fat and carbohydrate to energy is inefficient, with some 80% being given off as heat. At full gallop, the potential increase in body temperature is about 1 °C per minute. The main way the horse can dissipate this high heat load is through evaporative cooling. The primary means used by the horse is evaporation of sweat from the skin. A secondary means is evaporative cooling from the respiratory tract.

Horses are stunning sweaters. Sweating rates in humans of a mere 1.5 litres per hour have been reported. In contrast, the maximum rate in horses is 10 to 15 litres per hour! Quite clearly the sweating capacity of the horse is designed to cope with high heat loads. Horse sweat also contains a remarkable protein with the appropriate name of latherin, which is responsible for the frothy lather often seen on sweating horses. Latherin was isolated from horse sweat in 1986 by John Beeley and his colleagues in the Department of Biochemistry at the University of Glasgow. One of the properties of latherin is that it will stick to surfaces that are hydrophobic, or don't have a natural affinity with water, such as horse hair and skin. Latherin acts as a surfactant and promotes the spreading and evaporation of sweat. Loss of sweat in the form of droplets is clearly less efficient as a means of cooling than is spreading sweat over an animal's hair and skin. Hence, the muck lather on Stedamink helped her cool down.

Heat loss due to sweating has been estimated to reduce skin temperature by 2 to 4 °C. David Hodgson has pointed out that sweating rates in horses competing in long distance endurance races are often greater than what is needed to dissipate heat, resulting in sweat dripping from the horse. This can lead to problems with dehydration. If exercise continues so that heat dissipation mechanisms can no longer match those of heat production then muscle and core temperatures may approach critical levels. If exercise is performed at high ambient temperatures, particularly those above body temperature, and if relative humidity is high, then core temperatures are likely to reach these critical levels more quickly. Horses often produce more sweat when humidity is high, but as evaporation is impaired much of the sweat drips from the body and contributes little to cooling. The end result is a rapid onset of fatigue and possible heat stress.

An interesting fact for horse watchers is that training lowers the sweating threshold in humans. Although not confirmed, this effect is likely to occur in horses as well. Training would result in a more rapid onset of sweating and a slower increase in body temperature, so that performance time was prolonged. So on hot days, sweating up could be a good sign! Laura McCutcheon at the University of Guelph in Canada has found some evidence for this effect. In horses exposed to and exercised in hot humid conditions for 21 days the sweating threshold was reduced by about 1 °C.

But back to the causes of sweating. A horse sweats in response to thermal stimuli and stimulation of the sympathetic nervous system. Activation of the sympathetic nervous system is characteristic of the "fight-or-flight" response of many mammals. Nerve impulses pass to the adrenal glands and lead to increased production and release of the catecholamines - adrenalin and noradrenalin. Catecholamines cause a rise in heart rate, blood pressure and blood sugar. They prepare the animal for action, be it attack (fight) or escape (flight). In the horse, adrenalin causes an increase in sweating. So, the question is - Can you tell whether a horse is sweating because it is hot or nervous? Are there different areas of the body which are affected? One obvious area is between the horse's hind legs, where sweat is often visible when the rest of the body is dry. I suppose the equivalent situation in humans would be the association between sweaty palms and fear. These are excellent questions which I flashed off by email to Finola McConaghy. Finola replied that unfortunately horses have similar sweating patterns for both exercise and nervous sweating. Both seem to be associated with increased adrenalin. But if horses are sweating at moderate temperatures and show other signs of nervousness, then this could be a sign.

And that is the key. I try to think of sweating as an adrenalin response. The horse is prepared for action. If it's too aroused, then it is a bad sign. If it is too nervous or fearful, then that too is a bad sign. If a horse is calm, then sweating is cool! Remember Dane Ripper (*see* Chapter 1, page 10). Remember countless sweaters who go out and win.

In summary, I record in my race book if a horse is **Sweating** anywhere on its body on a scale of 1 to 3. I look in particular at the flank, under the saddlery, the neck, and the chest. I try to leave it till the last minute as the horses are stepping out onto the track, since what appears as light sweating in the flank in the parade ring can be full blown muck lather on the track. I use a score of 1 for light sweating, 2 for moderate, covering a large area of the body (Photo 50), and 3 if sweat is dripping off the horse or I see extensive latherin.

Photo 50
Montaigne Way, Sweating on the neck, back,
barrel and flank, before winning Race 2,
Flemington, 16 March 2002.

I score sweating between the hind legs separately. Some American horse watchers incorrectly refer to sweating in this area as kidney sweat. The horse's kidneys actually lie behind the ribcage under the spine, probably closest to the loin region (*see* Figure 2.1 on page 18), and nowhere near the hind legs. I don't know of a good slang term for sweat in this area, but I'm toying with a few possibilities - what about backside breakout, or bum scum? Again, I use three levels for **Hind leg sweating**. I use 1 for an area about the size of a fist, 2 for dinner plate size, and 3 if sweat is dripping down one hind leg (Photo 51). Invariably, because of friction, hind leg sweat is lathery. Sometimes horses are wet underneath and between the hind legs, but show no signs of latherin. This is usually because the trainer has given them a last-minute hose down. I'm generally suspicious of these horses and assign them a 3 for hind leg sweating.

There is no real need for me to use a scale of 1 to 3 for bodily fluid variables such as sweating, hind leg sweating and salivating. I do it out of habit and years spent trying to record a complete and accurate description of an animal's behaviour. But a simple measure of whether the horse is sweating or not would be quite adequate. Whenever I have compared the effect of say light or severe sweating on racing performance I have found no significant differences.

Photo 51
Fuji Dancer, Hind leg sweating,
Flemington, 16 March 2002.

Somewhere in my journey from the birdcage to the mounting yard I will usually hear the course broadcaster announce any rider weight changes. I always write in my book if a jockey is riding **Overweight**.

This is really a relic from our looksee study, but is quite a powerful variable in pointing to potential losers. The *Rules of Racing* allow for a jockey to ride half a kilogram overweight, but the stewards seem to allow up to 1 kilogram. There may be many reasons for a jockey being overweight, including an injury to the regular jockey requiring a last minute replacement. Or maybe the regular jockey had a big night at Smorgy's.

Photo 52
Flurry's Gem, Airborne jockey,
Moonee Valley, 23 December 2000.

But once the jockey is in the saddle, fat or thin, I first check that he or she stays there. Occasionally, you might be lucky enough to see an airborne jockey. At Moonee Valley one day I was photographing horses as they stepped onto the track. The four-year-old mare Flurry's Gem baulked right in front of me and sent the young apprentice Vincent Hall somersaulting in front of my lens. Click! It's nice to have a photograph of **Airborne jockey** (Photo 52). I have given it pride of place in my poolroom. Surprisingly, Flurry's Gem still finished second. Some horses obviously have a reputation for tossing their jockeys. The mare Piavonic is always led around the mounting yard riderless, with the jockey hopping on as she steps onto the track. I would like to record the behaviour of the horse as the jockey mounts, but my resources are spread too thinly. With a dozen or more jockeys mounting simultaneously I cannot watch each one to see if the horse is circling, remains stationary, or tries to move off. I still have an open mind on whether a horse moving off during mounting is a schooling fault or a potential indicator of poor performance.

With the jockey up I look again at the horse's head for any signs of resentment that the jockey is on board. I simply score head position as before, but now I call it **Head up - jockey up** (Photo 53). I also note whether the horse is still straining on the bit with **Neck twisted - jockey up**. This variable is a recent addition to my list of variables and so I don't know if it points to poor performance.

Photo 53
Tyson's Bite, Head up - jockey up,
Flemington, 12 May 2000.

As the horses are leaving the mounting yard I will note in my race book if a horse is **Grabbed by the clerk** (Photos 54 and 55). At Melbourne metropolitan meetings there are three clerks and in some races all three are flat out controlling unruly horses. The clerks grab

Photo 54
Unknown horse, Grabbed by clerk,
Flemington, 20 April 2002.

Photo 55
Real Boy, Grabbed by clerk,
Sandown, 17 March 2002.

the reins or bridle of a horse for many reasons. They know all the confirmed stirrers running around and will generally take preventative action as soon as they enter the yard. If a jockey is having trouble controlling a horse he may ask for help, or the trainer or jockey may ask for help even if the horse is not acting up and they want it to arrive at the barrier in a calm state. If the clerk grabs a horse with saddlecloth number 1 it is not necessarily a bad sign, since they normally lead the parade out together. If the clerk grabs the favourite, especially if it is short-priced, it too is not necessarily a bad sign. And often a clerk may give the horse a stroke or rub on the crest, which is very positive and to be encouraged. But, if you have been watching your selection in a race, and its head is up, its head is up with the jockey up, and it is grabbed by the clerk, head straight for the bar and do not bet. Increasing signs of arousal which are followed by control by the clerk are generally a very bad sign.

As the horses leave the mounting yard they may walk, trot or canter 200 metres or so down the track in the opposite direction from the barrier and then return at full speed in a warm-up gallop. Some horses omit this warm-up gallop altogether. It is easiest to notice them when the majority of horses turn left out of the yard, and those skiving on the warm-up turn right. I write **No warm-up** in my race book for these horses. Up until recently I didn't distinguish between the quality of the warm-up, and as long as a horse took the long way to the barrier I was happy. But I'm now thinking about recording whether a horse walks, canters or gallops in its warm-up.

My interest in no warm-up is in response to a fascinating study by Catherine Tyler and her colleagues at the University of Sydney. Catherine looked at the effect of a warm-up on energy supply during high intensity exercise. There are two main metabolic pathways used by horses to draw on energy during a horse race, anaerobic and aerobic. The anaerobic pathway involves the immediate breakdown of glycogen and build up of lactic acid in the muscles, leading to rapid fatigue. The aerobic pathway requires oxygen and takes longer to start up, but once it is going it can provide energy for a sustained effort. In the racehorse anaerobic metabolism is thought to be important in sprint races up to 1200 metres, and in distance races aerobic metabolism becomes more important. Cathy tested horses on a treadmill. Some were exercised at a speed equivalent to half their maximum oxygen uptake for 5 minutes, followed by 5 minutes walking. The others received no other warm-up and walked for 2 minutes. The horses were then accelerated on the treadmill to a speed equivalent to high intensity exercise. They were run just to the point of fatigue, which was when the horse was unable to keep up with the treadmill, despite encouragement. This lasted for 1 to 2 minutes. Horses that had received the warm-up had a greater proportion of their energy supplied by aerobic sources (79.3%) compared with horses that did not warm-up (72.4%). The main implication of this study is that a warm-up is likely to allow a greater use of aerobic energy sources and possibly delay the onset of fatigue. Hence, in distance races horses that haven't warmed up are likely to fatigue sooner. I mark in my race book **No warm-up** if a horse misses the normal warm-up routine and the race is 1600 metres or longer.

My penultimate variable is **Late**. Horses often arrive late on the track for various reasons. As mentioned in Chapter 2, many trainers try to hold their horses back in the birdcage until the last minute to reduce their exposure to the pre-race atmosphere and tension. Horses can also be late if there is a last minute change of jockey, or the horse needs to be replated in the stalls. Other horses may be late in arriving because the trainer or strapper has forgotten a vital piece of gear, or needs to make some last minute adjustment, or has left his packet of cigarettes in the stall. My criterion for deciding whether a horse is late is if the call to "Mount up please riders" has gone out from the stewards. If a horse is not in the mounting yard by then I regard it as a bad sign and note it in my race book. Occasionally, if a latecomer has a good excuse, I will make an exception. On big race days the trainer of the winner of a Group One race may get caught up in mounting yard celebrations and be late back to the birdcage if he has a horse entered in the next race. But still, be careful. The trainer may have had a couple of stiff whiskies in the Committee Room and over or under-tighten the girth strap! And occasionally the whole field can be late. If a horse has bolted in the previous race and has eluded capture in the car park for a long time, it can totally disrupt the next race. All horses may arrive late in the mounting yard and progress straight onto the track, with no opportunity for assessment.

Finally, now that the jockey has the horse on the track and is in total control, I have one last lingering look through my binoculars at the horse's head. Is it resisting? The horse may be fighting the jockey and tossing its head up, mouth open, or even refusing to go forwards. Any horse that does not proceed to the barrier in an orderly manner is marked in my book as **Resisting** (Photo 56).

Photo 56
Lady Camelot, Resisting,
Moonee Valley, 23 December 2000.

Many horses may play up once they get to the barrier, and refuse to enter in a calm manner, or require exceptional force from the barrier attendants. They may be blindfolded, have their ears or tail twisted, the jockey may need to dismount, or they may require special equipment such as a barrier blanket. They may break through the gates, or become cast in the stalls. But I'm afraid that by then it's all too late for me to record in my race book. I've already lined up to place my bet.

Chapter 11 60 variables and 10,509 horses

When I get home from a day at the races, and after I have handed over my winnings to The Missus, or alternatively explained in great detail the extraordinary circumstances that led to a totally inexplicable loss, I enter the day's results into my computer. I use a simple spreadsheet which has my current 65 variables across the top, one in each column, and a row for each horse. I then go through my race book horse by horse and record its behaviour in my spreadsheet by entering a "1" into the appropriate column if the horse performed the behaviour. Consider, for example, the scrawls in my race book for two horses who ran around in Race 2 at Moonee Valley on the 2 February 2001.

Horse number 9, Mr Lancelot, has 10 scrawled notes next to his name: Ring bit, Two hands, Head in, Head up, Stiff, Snort, Flare, Dump, Sweat 1, Hind leg sweat 1. Horse number 10, Orchestrated, has only one comment: Ring bit. I also enter the finishing position and starting price of each horse. Mr Lancelot finished fifth at $83.00 and Orchestrated finished second at $6.50.

Every month or so I check the total number of horses I have seen at the races and entered in this way into my database. When I last looked this was over 12,500 horses! However, before getting too carried away with this truly remarkable total you need to consider my attendance record at the races. I'm pretty much a fair weather sailor. I only go to Melbourne metropolitan meetings on a Saturday or public holiday. I don't bet on Sundays because it is against my religion, which quite categorically states:

> Thou shalt be allowed to bet six days a week but must rest comfortably on the seventh.

Also I don't go in the winter, when the tracks are wet, the weather is cold, and the horses have their rugs on. This usually means that my active period is from September through to May. I also have holidays at Christmas and Easter and I have been known to avoid days of extreme heat with those scorching Melbourne northerlies and temperatures of 40 degrees plus.

So, I average about 35 race meetings a year, looking at about 230 races and some 2800 entered horses. About 8-10% of entries are scratched, so I get to see about 2500 horses a year. The problem with this rate of accumulation of information is that by the time I have entered Horse number 12,500 into my spreadsheet it is probably about five years since I saw Horse number 1! This is really getting a bit long for the database to be regarded as up to date. In five years a lot can have happened to a horse watcher, and at the very least I've probably had two changes of prescription for my eyesight, and countless health check-ups. My definitions of horse behaviour could also have changed in that time and I will certainly have added some new variables and perhaps even have discarded some of the old ones. Ideally, a database should be large (more than 10,000 records) and recent (not more than two years old). It should also be dynamic, so that the new records replace the old. I've ended up settling on a compromise. My database is fairly large (about 10,000 records), is reasonably recent in an old sort of way (the last four years) and is dynamic (when I enter new records I toss out old ones).

Every now and then I talk to my database. Well, not literally, and I suppose the proper technical term is to "query" a database. But it is a very intense and deeply personal relationship. The Missus reckons that talking to me is sometimes like talking to a brick wall. That's usually because my mind is elsewhere, generally thinking up questions, sorry queries, for my database. What I usually ask is simply to add up all the columns, count the number of winners, and give me the strike rate for each variable. Here's the database's reply (Table 11.1). There were 11,443 horses entered into the 926 races that I watched over the four years between the Australian Cup

Table 11.1
Strike rates for 60 variables observed in 10,509 horses

Location	Variable	Number of winners	Number of starters	Strike rate (%)
Birdcage stalls	Pawing	131	1639	8.0
	Weaving	12	229	5.2
	Nibbling	36	410	8.8
	Kicking	11	167	6.6
	No strapper	25	324	7.7
	Pony	26	176	14.8
	Hand-held	41	480	8.5
	Positive strapper	16	183	8.7
Parade ring	Bit type - ring bit	451	5061	8.9
	Chewing	123	1134	10.8
	Grinding	40	448	8.9
	Neck twisted	96	1271	7.6
	Gaping	11	160	6.9
	Tongue tie	83	1008	8.2
	Lolling	18	207	8.7
	Licking	40	378	10.6
	Salivating	151	1347	11.2
	Crossover noseband	18	358	5.0
	Nose roll	15	197	7.6
	Pacifiers	21	257	8.2
	White eye	15	176	8.5
	Cannon bandages	15	203	7.4
	Tapes	97	1104	8.8
	Other bandages	2	74	2.7
Mounting yard	Two strappers	4	48	8.3
	Baulking	16	220	7.3
	Tugging	34	365	9.3
	Sloping strapper	61	535	11.4
	Two hands	44	552	8.0
	Shoulder	28	300	9.3
	Circling	7	106	6.6

Table 11.1 (continued)

Location	Variable	Number of winners	Number of starters	Strike rate (%)
Mounting yard	Positive strapper	28	271	10.3
	Negative strapper	0	12	0.0
	Strapper remarks	5	64	7.8
	Slow gait	14	261	5.4
	Fast gait	14	210	6.7
	Changing gait	137	1613	8.5
	Bucking	14	213	6.6
	Prancing	35	309	11.3
	Short stride	47	447	10.5
	Head up	268	3142	8.5
	Head in	124	1164	10.7
	Head out	71	693	10.2
	Ears side or back	150	1847	8.1
	Ears flicking	66	776	8.5
	Tail stiff or swished	252	2762	9.1
	Tail flat	10	106	9.4
	Tail flared	57	655	8.7
	Dumping	52	636	8.2
	Sex signs	4	53	7.5
	Snorting	67	738	9.1
	Whinnying	4	41	9.8
Track	Sweating	155	1621	9.6
	Hind leg sweating	116	1046	11.1
	Overweight jockey	6	113	5.3
	Head up - jockey up	121	1407	8.6
	Grabbed by clerk	94	1119	8.4
	No warm-up	15	154	9.7
	Late	7	134	5.2
	Resisting	22	316	7.0
	All horses	932	10509	8.9
	Favourites	281	926	30.3

meeting in March 1998 and March 2002. Nine hundred and thirty-four horses were scratched leaving 10,509 horses that were actually observed. Nine hundred and thirty-two of these 10,509 horses won, which is a strike rate of 8.9%. If you are wondering how 932 horses can win 926 races the answer is that there were six dead heats. The average field size was 11.3 horses (10,509/926=11.3). So the chance of a horse winning, on average, is one chance in 11.3 chances, or 0.089. In other words, the chance of any horse winning a race is the same as the strike rate for all horses of 8.9%. Favourites won 281 of the 926 races, a strike rate of 30.3%. So favourites win much more than expected by chance. In fact, this statistic, that favourites win 30% of all races, has remained remarkably constant since humans first started betting on racehorses. Despite all the advances in technology over the thousands of years since a metal bar was first placed in a horse's mouth, the ability of the public to pick a winner is unchanged!

I saw 1639 horses **Pawing** the ground in the birdcage. One hundred and thirty-one of these horses won, a strike rate of 8.0%. So, pawing horses win less often than you would expect by chance alone. The strike rates for 60 of my current 65 variables are shown, and range from a low of 0.0% for **Negative strapper** up to 14.8% for **Pony**. But a brief word of warning. If the number of starters is less than 100 we need to be a bit careful as the sample size may not be large enough for an accurate measure of strike rate. For some variables, the sample size may be small because they have been added relatively recently to my original list of 50 variables. Examples are **Two strappers** and **Strapper remarks**, which I have only been scoring for two years. For other variables, the sample size may be small because they are such rare events. Examples are **Negative strapper**, **Other bandages**, **Whinnying**, and **Sex signs**, all of which I have been scoring since 1997. I have excluded five of my current 65 variables from Table 11.1 because they have sample sizes less than 100 and because they have been added to my list within the last year. These variables are **Restless**, **Flared nostrils**, **Neck arched**, **Neck twisted - jockey up**, and **Clacking**.

The strike rates for individual variables, whilst extremely interesting, are not much use in that form. You have to continually compare them with the average strike rate of 8.9%. A simple and straightforward way around this problem is to compare the observed number of winners with the number expected by chance alone. So for **Pawing** horses, the expected number of winners is the number of starters who were pawing (1639) multiplied by the average chance of winning (932/10,509 or 8.9%), which gives 145.4. Subtracting the expected number of winners from the actual observed number of winners gives a difference of -14.4. So pawing horses win 14.4 races less than expected. In order to compare this figure with other variables I express it as a percentage by dividing it by the number of expected winners. So, 100*(-14.4/145.4) = -10%. Pawing horses win 10% less often than expected by chance.

In Table 11.2 I give the % disadvantages (or advantages) for all 60 variables. You will immediately notice that some variables are negative, some are positive, and some hardly have an impact. To make this more apparent and immediately useful I have rearranged them in rank order in Table 11.3.

As Paul Keating would say, what a beautiful set of numbers. Some of these results are truly wonderful and confirm all my gut feelings about bad horse behaviour. Look at horses that are **Fast**, **Slow** or **Late**! Look at **Bucking** and **Kicking**. Look at horses with their **Necks twisted**, with **Tongue ties**, and **Gaping**! Look at horses **Weaving** in the birdcage! Look at **Other bandages**. Wouldn't Rem Plante be chuffed. Look at horses with **Nose rolls**! How on earth did Taufan's Melody win?

But we shouldn't be too surprised. After all, I started out looking for negative variables. So, it's probably more worthwhile to scan the Neutral and Positive variables and see if there are any possible explanations for why these variables were not negative. **Bit type**, for example, is absolutely neutral. This is no surprise since the ring bit is supposed to keep the horse on course, and should be neither negative

Table 11.2
Percentage disadvantage/advantage for 60 variables

Location	Variable	Observed number of winners (O)	Expected number of winners (E)	Difference (O-E)	Disadvantage (O-E)/E %
Birdcage	Pawing	131	145.4	-14.4	-10
	Weaving	12	20.3	-8.3	-41
	Nibbling	36	36.4	-0.4	-1
	Kicking	11	14.8	-3.8	-26
	No strapper	25	28.7	-3.7	-13
	Pony	26	15.6	10.4	67
	Hand-held	41	42.6	-1.6	-4
	Positive strapper	16	16.2	-0.2	-1
Ring	Bit type - ring bit	451	448.8	2.2	0
	Chewing	123	100.6	22.4	22
	Grinding	40	39.7	0.3	1
	Neck twisted	96	112.7	-16.7	-15
	Gaping	11	14.2	-3.2	-22
	Tongue tie	83	89.4	-6.4	-7
	Lolling	18	18.4	-0.4	-2
	Licking	40	33.5	6.5	19
	Salivating	151	119.5	31.5	26
	Cr-over noseband	18	31.7	-13.7	-43
	Nose roll	15	17.5	-2.5	-14
	Pacifiers	21	22.8	-1.8	-8
	White eye	15	15.6	-0.6	-4
	Cannon bandages	15	18.0	-3.0	-17
	Tapes	97	97.9	-0.9	-1
	Other bandages	2	6.6	-4.6	-70
Yard	Two strappers	4	4.3	-0.3	-6
	Baulking	16	19.5	-3.5	-18
	Tugging	34	32.4	1.6	5
	Sloping strapper	61	47.4	13.6	29
	Two hands	44	49.0	-5.0	-10
	Shoulder	28	26.6	1.4	5

Table 11.2 (continued)

Location	Variable	Observed number of winners (O)	Expected number of winners (E)	Difference (O-E)	Disadvant- age (O-E)/E %
Yard	Circling	7	9.4	-2.4	-26
	Positive strapper	28	24.0	4.0	17
	Negative strapper	0	1.1	-1.1	-100
	Strapper remarks	5	5.7	-0.7	-12
	Slow gait	14	23.1	-9.1	-40
	Fast gait	14	18.6	-4.6	-25
	Changing gait	137	143.1	-6.1	-4
	Bucking	14	18.9	-4.9	-26
	Prancing	35	27.4	7.6	28
	Short stride	47	39.6	7.4	19
	Head up	268	278.7	-10.7	-4
	Head in	124	103.2	20.8	20
	Head out	71	61.5	9.5	16
	Ears side or back	150	163.8	-13.8	-8
	Ears flicking	66	68.8	-2.8	-4
	Tail stiff or swished	252	245.0	7.0	3
	Tail flat	10	9.4	0.6	6
	Tail flared	57	58.1	-1.1	-2
	Dumping	52	56.4	-4.4	-8
	Sex signs	4	4.7	-0.7	-15
	Snorting	67	65.5	1.5	2
	Whinnying	4	3.6	0.4	10
Track	Sweating	155	143.8	11.2	8
	Hind leg sweating	116	92.8	23.2	25
	Overweight jockey	6	10.0	-4.0	-40
	Head up -jockey up	121	124.8	-3.8	-3
	Grabbed by clerk	94	99.2	-5.2	-5
	No warm-up	15	13.7	1.3	10
	Late	7	11.9	-4.9	-41
	Resisting	22	28.0	-6.0	-21

Table 11.3
Percentage disadvantage/advantage in rank order

Effect on chance of winning	Variable	Disadvantage/ Advantage %
Negative	Negative strapper	-100
	Other bandages	-70
	Crossover noseband	-43
	Late	-41
	Weaving	-41
	Overweight jockey	-40
	Slow gait	-40
	Circling	-26
	Bucking	-26
	Kicking	-26
	Fast gait	-25
	Gaping	-22
	Resisting	-21
	Baulking	-18
	Cannon bandages	-17
	Sex signs	-15
	Neck twisted	-15
	Nose roll	-14
	No strapper	-13
	Strapper remarks	-12
	Two hands	-10
	Pawing	-10
	Ears side or back	-8
	Pacifiers	-8
	Dumping	-8
	Tongue tie	-7
	Two strappers	-6
	Grabbed by clerk	-5
	Changing gait	-4

Table 11.3 (continued)

© Geoffrey Hutson 2002

Effect on chance of winning	Variable	Disadvantage/ Advantage %
Negative	Ears flicking	-4
	White eye	-4
	Head up	-4
	Hand-held	-4
	Head up - jockey up	-3
Neutral	Lolling	-2
	Tail flared	-2
	Positive strapper (stalls)	-1
	Nibbling	-1
	Tapes	-1
	Bit type - ring bit	0
	Grinding	1
	Snorting	2
Positive	Tail stiff or swished	3
	Tugging	5
	Shoulder	5
	Tail flat	6
	Sweating	8
	No warm-up	10
	Whinnying	10
	Head out	16
	Positive strapper (yard)	17
	Short stride	19
	Licking	19
	Head in	20
	Chewing	22
	Hind leg sweating	25
	Salivating	26
	Prancing	28
	Sloping strapper	29
	Pony	67

nor positive. I simply record it in order to focus my mind on the horse and my pen on the race book. Similarly, **Tapes**, are meant to prevent injury to the bumpers and shouldn't be masking any serious problem such as a dodgy tendon or any other injury. I wasn't surprised that that **Snorting** was neutral, since it seems to be a demonstrative sound. I am disappointed that both **Grabbed by the clerk** and **Head up - jockey up** are only mildly negative, since our pilot study suggested that these were important variables.

Of the positive variables, many are exactly what you would expect. **Pony**, the bestest positive, suggests that caring and compassionate trainers can reap the rewards. The bodily fluid variables **Sweating**, **Hind leg sweating**, **Salivating** and their associated behaviours, **Licking** and **Chewing** are all positive. I have already mentioned that sweating on its own is not an indicator of poor performance. An interesting cluster of positive variables is **Tugging**, **Sloping strapper**, **Shoulder**, **Short stride**, **Head in**, **Head out** and **Prancing**. These variables all describe the big, dominant, strong horse, that the strapper is struggling to contain. The American horseplayer Joe Takach describes these types of horses as "ready to win" and quite clearly they are. Unfortunately, these horses are not much use to me in general since I'm trying to rule horses out, not rule them in. I want to bet on horses with a clean sheet, and these horses have so many variables scored next to their name in my race book that I find it hard to back them. But I am wary of them, and respect them greatly. The main shocks in the positive list are **Whinnying** and **No warm-up**. **No Warm-up** can possibly be explained since I record it regardless of race distance and it is probably only important in distance races. **Whinnying** seems to be a contact call and its occurrence may not indicate undue fear or alarm. However, the sample size is small and I will probably need to record it for a few more years to be sure.

Averages can be very misleading. Statisticians will tell you that if you have one hand in a bucket of boiling water and the other in a bucket of ice, then on average you are at a comfortable temperature.

It is much the same when considering individual behaviour variables. Consider the variable **Hand-held**, in the birdcage stalls. A horse might be hand-held because it is going berserk in the stalls. Or it might be hand-held because the trainer and strapper are aware of the calming effects of close human contact on their horse, and are endeavouring to present the horse in the yard as relaxed as possible. On average, if there are equal numbers of berserk and calm horses, then **Hand-held** would show up as a neutral variable. (In fact, it was slightly negative, so there must be more berserk ones). One way around this problem is to consider more than one variable at a time, and do, say, a multivariate analysis, such as multiple regression. However, that could frighten the horses, not to mention the horse watchers, and is beyond the scope of this book. Another way could be to look at the advantage/disadvantage of pairs of variables. With 60 variables, there are 1770 pairs of variables, so this could be a long process. If you wanted to look at triplets, there are 34,220 combinations, which is a very long process. If you wanted to look at quads, well, it all gets too complicated.

So, I think the simplest solution is just to add up the percentages for all the negative variables. For example, if a horse is hand-held, and goes berserk in the mounting yard, it will have an entry in my race book something like this:

> Birdcage: Pawing, Hand-held
> Parade ring: Salivating
> Mounting yard: Two hands, Changing gait, Bucking, Head up, Head out, Ears side, Tail stiff, Tail flared, Dumping
> Track: Head up - jockey up, Grabbed by clerk

Adding up the percentages for this horse's expected disadvantage we get:

> Birdcage: 10+4
> Parade ring: 0
> Mounting yard: 10+4+26+4+0+8+0+0+8
> Track: 3+5

for a total score of 82%. Horses of this type will win 82% less often than expected by chance. Notice that I ignore any neutral or positive variables like salivating and flared tail.

The horse that is hand-held in the stalls and is relaxed will have an entry in my race book like this:

> Birdcage: Hand-held, Positive
> Parade ring: Salivating
> Mounting yard: Positive
> Track: OK

Adding up the percentages for this horse's expected disadvantage we get:

> Birdcage: 4+0
> Parade ring: 0
> Mounting yard: 0
> Track: 0

for a total score of 4%. Horses of this type will win 4% less often than expected by chance.

The total percentage disadvantage can be regarded as a bad behaviour score. But, probably the simplest way to think of it is as a horse's **Behavioural handicap!** In the same way that horses can be handicapped by weight, they can be handicapped by their own behaviour. A horse's behavioural handicap is the sum of the percentage disadvantage for each individual negative variable. And it provides an instant measure of whether a horse will win less than expected by chance.

Now the obvious question to ask is: "Do the good guys win?" So, I asked my database and it gave me a fascinating answer (Figure 11.1).

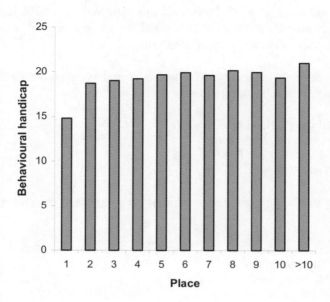

Figure 11.1
Average behavioural handicaps for all finishing positions.

The average behavioural handicap of winners was 14.6, the average of second through to ninth ranged from 18.7 to 20.1 and the average of tenth or worse was 21.0. The good guys, the winners, are clearly, on average, a better-behaved bunch of horses than the losers. But averages, as we already know, can cover up a lot of interesting information. So I asked my database, the same question, but in a different way. "What is the relationship between a horse's chance of winning and its behavioural handicap?" And now it gave up the results for 10,509 horses, with a horse's chance of winning, or strike rate, classified according to its behavioural handicap (Figure 11.2).

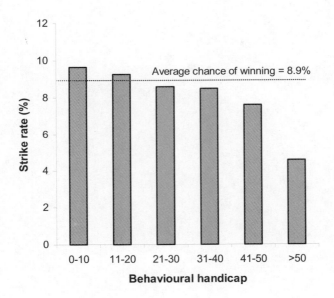

Figure 11.2
Effect of behavioural handicap on chance of winning (strike rate).

Horses with a behavioural handicap of 10 or less won 9.7% of races. Horses with a handicap of between 11 and 20 won 9.3% of races. Both these strike rates are greater than the strike rate of 8.9% expected by chance. In other words, horses with a behavioural handicap of less than 20 win more than expected by chance. As the behavioural handicap increases above 20, then horses become more likely to lose. If the behavioural handicap is greater than 50, horses win half as much as expected by chance. In other words, they are twice as likely to lose.

And that is the key to behavioural handicapping. As bad behaviour increases, so does a horse's losing chance.

Chapter 12 Betting on behaviour

At last it's time to have a bet. All this horse watching tends to give me an itchy wallet. But first, before reaching for the bankroll, I have to make my selections. I can best illustrate how I do this with an example. Let's consider the Carlyon Cup, a 1600 metre Group Two race, run at Caulfield on 17 February 2001. My race book looked something like Table 12.1.

My selections in this race were TAB numbers 2, 3, 6 and 11. Since I am working very quickly I generally cross out horses as soon as I see something wrong with them. Remember, I am looking for cleanskins, horses with no behavioural handicaps, but I am prepared to accept horses with one or two minor faults. A rough and ready method is simply to cross out a horse if it has two or more black marks, or negative variables, written next to its name. In this race I crossed out numbers 1, 4, 5 (the favourite), 7, 8, 9 and 10. The topweight and eventual winner, Northerly, looked very keen, so much so that I had written "Aroused" in my race book. This horse was not fractious, tossing its head up, changing gait, and rearing, but needed strong control from both the strapper and clerk. Another hint that he was not fractious was that, although his tail was flared, he did not dump. The two horse, Oval Office, was beautiful, hand-held in the stall with a positive, stroking strapper. More strapper stroking in the yard. A standout selection, with no behavioural handicap. Iron Horse was a bit of a worry. Hand-held in the birdcage, taken in hand by the clerk, and sweating. The six, Shining Path, was a query horse. No visible strapper on the first trip past his stall, hand-held on the second. The eleven, Knockroe, looked terrific.

If you like arithmetic, a more precise method is to calculate each horse's behavioural handicap using percentages. I have done this in Table 12.2.

Table 12.1
Appearance of horses in the Carlyon Cup, 1600 metres,
Caulfield, 17 February 2001

TAB	Horse	Birdcage	Ring	Yard	Track
1	**Northerly**	Paw	Cheekers	Slope 2 hands Fast Tail stiff Tail flared "Aroused"	Clerk
2	**Oval Office**	Positive Hand-held	Positive		
3	**Shorblue**		Ring bit Chew Tongue tie Tapes	Sweat 1	
4	**Furnish**	Paw	Ring bit Positive	Ears side Tail stiff Tail flared Dump	
5	**Play Station**		Ring bit Neck twisted	Head up Tail flared Dump Snort	
6	**Shining Path**	Paw No strapper Hand-held	Ring bit	Ears side HLsweat 2	
7	**Iron Horse**	Hand-held		Sweat 2 HLsweat 2	Clerk
8	**Tiger's Eye**			Sweat 1	Head up Resist
9	**Collins Street**	Scratched			
10	**Kensign**		Neck twisted	Head in Head out Ears back Tail stiff	Head up
11	**Knockroe**	Paw	Ring bit	Lick	

Table 12.2
Behavioural handicaps of horses in the Carlyon Cup, 1600 metres,
Caulfield, 17 February 2001

TAB	Horse	Birdcage	Ring	Yard	Track	Total
1	Northerly	10	0	35	5	50
2	Oval Office	4	0			4
3	Shorblue		7	0		7
4	Furnish	10	0	16		26
5	Play Station		15	12		27
6	Shining Path	27	0	8		35
7	Iron Horse	4		0	5	9
8	Tiger's Eye			0	25	25
9	Collins Street	Scr	-	-	-	-
10	Kensign	0	15	8	3	26
11	Knockroe	10	0	0	0	10

This method gives much the same results, and if the cut-off line is drawn at 20%, as indicated in Chapter 11, it suggests that Shining Path should be left out and Iron Horse put in.

After making my selections I transferred the numbers to the blank page at the back of my race book where there's a bit of space to do some quick calculations. I then consulted the tote screen for the approximate win dividends and wrote them down next to each horse's number (Table 12.3).

Table 12.3
Horse watcher's market for the Carlyon Cup, 1600 metres,
Caulfield, 17 February 2001

TAB	Win dividend ($)	Comment	Bet to win $100 ($)
2	5.90	B	17
3	6.10		17
6	14.00		8
11	26.80		4
		Total outlay to win $100	46

I also write next to each selection's TAB number whether it is the favourite (marked with an F), my best selection with the best behavioural handicap (marked with a B) or a long shot paying more than $30 for a win (marked with an L). I then work out how much I would have to bet to win $100 on each of these horses simply by dividing the tote win dividend for each horse into 100. Adding these up I see that I would have to outlay $46 to bet on all four horses and collect $100 if any of the four won. If the total amount I need to outlay is less than $65 I generally have a bet. The $65 is an arbitrary amount, but I figure that if a winner will return at least half my bet, then it is a reasonable risk. At the moment I am betting solely for the place on the favourite, if it's showing $1.50 or more. If the favourite has been eliminated or is showing $1.40 or less on the place tote, then I bet on the horse with the best behavioural handicap. In this race that was obviously Oval Office, who finished second at $1.80. It was a strong win by the top weight, Northerly, the keen horse in the yard, and an excellent third by Knockroe.

Not all races are as straight forward as the Carlyon Cup with a standout selection and an obvious bet. Some races I end up crossing

Table 12.4
Appearance of horses in the International Exchange Race Day Handicap,
1400 metres, Caulfield, 17 February 2001

TAB	Horse	Birdcage	Ring	Yard	Track
1	**Brew**		Ring bit		Sweat 1
2	**Typhoon**		Ring/soft bit Pacifiers	Tail stiff	
3	**Jumallique**	Paw	Chew	Head in	No warm-up
4	**Logical Reason**		Tongue tie		
5	**Dylan**			Ears back Tail stiff	HLsweat 3
6	**Ken Cheval**	Paw Hand-held	Nose roll Salivate 1	Ch gait	HLsweat 2
7	**Slalom**		Ring bit	Ears side	
8	**Emission**				Sweat 1 Over
9	**Mamoloni**		Ring bit	Ear flick Ears side Tail stiff	Head up
10	**Teddy Bear**	Nibble Hand-held	Ring bit Salivate 1	Ch gait Head up Ears side	Head up HLsweat 3

out all horses. Other races I can't cross out any. They all look terrific.
For example, my race book for the get-out stakes on Carlyon Cup
day looked something like Table 12.4. I could only cross out four
horses, the 6, 8, 9 and 10. The behavioural handicaps are shown in
Table 12.5.

The main difference from my rough and ready method was
Mamoloni, who didn't quite reach the 20% cut off point. With or

Table 12.5
Behavioural handicaps of horses in the International Exchange Race Day
Handicap, 1400 metres, Caulfield, 17 February 2001

TAB	Horse	Birdcage	Ring	Yard	Track	Total
1	Brew		0		0	0
2	Typhoon		8	0		8
3	Jumallique	10	0	0	0	10
4	Logical Reason		7			7
5	Dylan			8	0	8
6	Ken Cheval	14	14	4	0	32
7	Slalom		0	8		8
8	Emission				40	40
9	Mamoloni		0	12	3	15
10	Teddy Bear	4	0	16	3	23

without Mamoloni, the market I calculated in the back of my race
book clearly pointed to no bet (Table 12.6).

I would have to outlay $87 to get $100 back, which is the fast track
to bankruptcy. If this was a bettable race, with a market outlay of $65
or less, my bet would have gone on the favourite, Logical Reason,
which finished second, paying $1.90 for the place. The best-behaved
horse in the race was Cup winner Brew, who had no faults, but
finished ninth of the 10 runners. The eventual winner was Emission,
whose jockey was riding half a kilogram overweight. On its own this
is not a serious crime, but in conjunction with other indicators of

Table 12.6
Horse watcher's market for the International Exchange Race
Day Handicap, 1400 metres, Caulfield, 17 February 2001

TAB	Win dividend ($)	Comment	Bet to win $100 ($)
1	11.40	B	9
2	5.60		18
3	8.40		12
4	4.90	F	21
5	9.70		11
7	8.20		13
9	36.30	L	3
	Total outlay to win $100		87

poor performance tends to be the straw that breaks the camel's back. Emission looked good, and obviously had no trouble with the extra half kilo.

The best thing about behavioural handicaps is that I am crossing horses out. And I don't have to know specifically what is wrong with the horse if it has shown me signs of bad behaviour. For example, a horse might be tossing its head up because the bit is not adjusted correctly in its mouth, or the tongue tie is too tight, or it is fearful, or it is overaroused, or it is overtrained. The precise cause of the behaviour, whilst very interesting, is of no practical significance for punting. It is a bit like modern motoring. We don't need to understand the workings of the internal combustion engine to accept that it will propel us forwards. It is much the same with the horse's mind. We don't need to be a horse psychologist to accept that there is a strong link between a horse's mental attitude, its behaviour, and racing performance.

The world's expert on horse body language and premier American horsewoman is the late, Bonnie Ledbetter. Together with Tom Ainslie, Bonnie has described all the different types of horse you are likely to see at the races - the sharp horse, the ready horse, the dull horse, the frightened horse, the angry horse, the hot horse, the cold horse, and the hurting horse. Bonnie reckoned that sharp, ready and dull horses won 90% of all races. She may well be right. But problems arise for apprentice horse watchers in trying to identify these particular types of horses. And what do you do when horses are only a little bit sharp, or the whole field is dull? Fun lovers and partygoers will find it much easier to identify particular behaviour patterns. They will also find it much easier to rule horses out than rule horses in.

In most races I would end up with between two and six horses. Sometimes none, when I cross them all out, sometimes only one, a standout selection. If B for best and F for favourite are written beside the same horse, I increase my bet. And if B for best and L for long shot are written beside the same horse, I increase my bet with some anticipation and alacrity. I generally would have four to six bets on an eight-race card, rarely none, and rarely eight. Average five. In a year I will average 175 bets.

I never bother lining up to collect after a race, but generally cash in all my winning tickets at the end of the day. And I never tear up any tickets at the track. Much better to wait until the tumult and the shouting has died and tear them up in the privacy of my own home. Besides, you need two hands to tear up tote tickets at the races, and one of my hands is always holding either a pen, a race book or a beer.

The other thing you will notice about my betting behaviour is that I bet on the totalisator. There are several reasons for this. The main one is that I don't trust bookmakers. This probably goes back to the running of the Second Commerce Novice at Eagle Farm on 18 August 1984. In case you have forgotten the details, Richard

Waterhouse, a historian at the University of Sydney (and no relation to the bookmaking family), has given a full account of this infamous affair. The ineptness of the perpetrators of the Fine Cotton substitution was laughable, but the involvement of prominent bookmaker Robbie Waterhouse was deplorable. He was found to have bet on the ring-in with prior knowledge, although he was not involved in the actual ring-in itself. Just as we were all starting to forget this scandal and put our toes back in the betting ring, Robbie was caught offering the extravagant odds of 500/1 about favourites to his employee and former Canberra bookmaker, Peter McCoy. No wonder I'm circumspect.

And it's not just Sydney bookies. Andrew Eddy has reported that one of Melbourne's most prominent bookmakers, Michael Eskander, was fined $5,000 for taking fake bets on the Call of the Card on Cup Eve. And these weren't small fake bets either, but involved an apparent outlay of $90,000 to win $700,000.

In addition to my fundamental misgivings about bookmakers, I often don't have the time to dash out into the ring and search for the best odds. If I'm betting on a favourite I may have a quick squiz around, but generally the tote pays better than the books for anything showing about $5.00 or more for a win. And I also think that tote odds are fairer, with their fixed percentage takeout. The machine is incorruptible, isn't it? Bookies at times offer such outrageous percentages that it is no surprise to find that they are headed for oblivion. And furthermore, why should I fund their gold watches in retirement? My gambling bank is invested in Tabcorp shares, so that at least if I lose I can still get some back through the annual dividends. I suppose I could ring up Mark Read's bookmaking outfit, International All Sports, because I've got shares in them too, but, it's a lot of fuss.

Besides, I always like to pay my respects to that great Australian scientific hero, George Julius, the inventor of the automatic totalisator. It is most important that we pause for a moment and pay tribute to George Julius's achievement. Both Brian Conlon and Stephanie Pain have given vivid descriptions of his remarkable life. He was born in Norwich, England in 1873 and was taken to Ballarat in 1884 where his father was appointed archdeacon. He loved helping his father in the workshop out the back, fixing and tinkering with broken clocks. In 1890 the family moved to Christchurch, New Zealand, where the old man had been kicked upstairs and installed as the bishop. Young George studied mechanical engineering at the university. In 1896 he scored his first job, working in Western Australia with the railways as a locomotive engineer. In his spare time he built an automatic vote counting machine to counter problems with rigged vote counting in local elections. The machine worked, but the voting system was changed, making the machine redundant. Julius moved to Sydney as an engineering consultant, but he was reluctant to give up his machine. He adapted it to solve a problem plaguing horse racing - doing the sums on the tote. Keeping track of the amounts invested on the tote was all done by hand and calculating dividends was so slow and time consuming that it wasn't always finished before the next race had started. In 1912 Julius took a working model of his machine on a world tour, and in 1913 the first full-size totalisator was installed at Ellerslie Park racecourse, in Auckland, New Zealand. The machine was ginormous, and occupied an entire building. It was totally mechanical, with pulleys, cogs and bicycle chains, and driven by cast iron weights which were hoisted up to the top of the building before the race meeting. The bets taken by each operator were fed to a mechanical adder, and then to the central totalisator. The totalisator summed bets from dozens of adders and drove a series of indicators which showed how much was bet on each horse. Julius returned to Sydney and set up Automatic Totalisators Limited and proceeded to sell totalisators to racetracks around the world. And he went on to become the first chairman of our premier scientific research establishment, the CSIRO. The last surviving Julius totalisator, an electro-mechanical machine at Harringay Stadium, a dog track in North London, was decommissioned on 25 September 1987, after 57 years of service.

What a shame that our lives haven't overlapped. Sir George Julius died on the 28 June 1946, the year before I was born. I dips me lid. The model Julius machine that George carted around the world is in the Powerhouse Museum, Sydney (Photo 57). It is an Aussie icon the equal of Phar Lap. You must visit it and pay your respects.

Photo 57
The George Julius model totalisator
(reproduced courtesy of the Powerhouse Museum, Sydney).

Where was I? Ah, yes, not tearing up tickets. There are a couple of other things that partygoers and fun lovers need to know about totalisators. Complete novices, who have never had a bet in their lives, should read Alan Aitken's excellent introduction *Hats in the Ring*. So off to the library with you, and come back later. Those who have collected a winning bet at least once in their lives are fortunately familiar with the concept of a dividend, and can read on. We don't have to worry about bookmakers' markets, and all that

Table 12.7
Win totalisator market for the Carlyon Cup, 1600 metres,
Caulfield, 17 February 2001

Horse	Win dividend ($)	Bet needed to win $100	Chance of winning (%)	Recalculated total amounts bet ($)	Recalculated exact dividend ($)
Northerly	4.80	20.83	17.68	109,279	4.8361
Oval Office	4.80	20.83	17.68	109,279	4.8361
Shorblue	6.40	15.63	13.26	81,959	6.4481
Furnish	21.00	4.76	4.04	24,978	21.1579
Play Station	3.20	31.25	26.52	163,919	3.2241
Shining Path	12.90	7.75	6.58	40,662	12.9970
Iron Horse	67.30	1.49	1.26	7,794	67.8060
Tiger's Eye	10.50	9.52	8.08	49,956	10.5789
Collins Street	Scr	-	-	-	-
Kensign	44.90	2.23	1.89	11,682	45.2376
Knockroe	28.20	3.55	3.01	18,601	28.4120
Totals		117.84	100.00	618,110	

scary stuff like odds, percentages and probabilities. We bet on the Julius machine, and all we have to worry about is how much we put in, and how much we take out. But, beware, bookmakers are trying to look more and more like totalisators and are trying seduce us by displaying what they call "decimal odds", which are in fact win dividends.

The two things about totalisators that we need to come to terms with are the **Take** and market **Fluctuations**.

A horse race market is simply a collection of opinions. The opinions of form analysts, weight raters, time handicappers, lucky number punters, jockey followers, horse watchers, owners, trainers, professionals, amateurs, drunks and derelicts. I stick my money on my opinion, the totalisator adds up the money on my opinion and everyone else's opinion, takes its cut off the top, currently around 14.5% for the win and 14.25% for the place, and returns the rest to the winning opinion. Simple, really. What a pity that the French, those Pacific pirates, get the credit for inventing it.

Let's look at the market of opinions for the Carlyon Cup (Table 12.7). Northerly, the winner, paid $4.80 for the win. In order to win $100 on Northerly I needed to invest 100/4.80, or $20.83. Adding up the amounts I needed to invest on all horses in order to win $100 no matter who won you can see that I would need to outlay $117.84. The $17.84 is the TAB's take or cut which it will keep after giving me my $100 back. You can work out how much the TAB takes as a percentage simply by dividing 17.84 by 117.84, i.e. 17.84/117.84 = 15.14%. This is 0.64% above the 14.5% that Tabcorp says it takes out of the win pool. This extra 0.64%, which varies from race to race, comes from rounding down, or what are known as fractions. The TAB, the miserable mongrel, keeps the fractions.

You can get a feel for the impact of fractions by recalculating the total amounts wagered on each horse, which I have shown in Table 12.7. To do this I worked out each horse's chance of winning, which is the bet needed to win $100 expressed as a percentage. In Northerly's case this is 100*(20.83/117.84) or 17.68%. The total win pool on the Carlyon Cup was $618,110. So the amount wagered on Northerly was 17.68% of this, or $109,279. Since 14.5% was skimmed off the win pool, this left $528,484 to hand back to Northerly punters. So, the exact dividend they should receive for $1

Table 12.8
Place totalisator market for the Carlyon Cup, 1600 metres,
Caulfield, 17 February 2001

Horse	Place dividend ($)	Bet needed to win $100	Recalculated exact dividend
Northerly	1.90	52.63	1.9527
Oval Office	1.80	55.56	1.8499
Shorblue	1.80	55.56	1.8499
Furnish	5.00	20.00	5.1386
Play Station	1.50	66.67	1.5416
Shining Path	3.10	32.26	3.1859
Iron Horse	10.20	9.80	10.4827
Tiger's Eye	2.90	34.48	2.9804
Collins Street	Scr	-	-
Kensign	8.50	11.76	8.7356
Knockroe	4.80	20.83	4.9331
Totals		359.55	

is \$528,484/109,279 = \$4.8361. The declared dividend was rounded down to \$4.80, leaving the extra 3.6 cents in Tabcorp's pocket. These estimates of the exact dividend are not totally precise, and tend to be less accurate above about \$15. But they give you the idea. The value of the fractions to Tabcorp and the loss to winning punters was 109,279*3.61 cents = \$3944.

The significance for fun punters of a take from the win pool of about 15 to 15.5% is that this is the amount you can expect to lose on average in any one year. If I outlay $25,000 a year I can only expect to get $21,125 back. My fun will cost me $3,875! So, the bottom line is that the totalisator take, including the fractions, is the price you pay for fun!

You probably think you are better off betting for the place, where the take is only 14.25% with Tabcorp. Think again. The problem with the place is that as the dividends get smaller the fractions gets bigger. If I wanted to collect $100 on each horse that was placed in the Carlyon Cup I would need to outlay $359.55 (Table 12.8). The TAB take is 59.55/359.55 = 16.6%. Let me say that again. A whopping 16.6%. The fractions on the smaller place dividends are worth an extra 2.35%. My calculations of the exact place dividend are probably accurate up to about $4.00. The place pool on the Carlyon Cup was $287,046, so the take on fractions was $6,745! What can we do about this despicable state of affairs? Well, we can whinge and moan, complain to Tabcorp, write letters to Mr Hulls, and in the meantime try to have more fun at the races. Get more bang for our buck.

The second thing to be wary about with totalisators is the fluctuations in approximate dividends. Everyone is trying to bet in the last few minutes before the jump so that they can follow the late mail, those-in-the-know, the so-called smart money. An avalanche of money into the pool can lead to some dramatic fluctuations in approximate dividends. Even after the horses have jumped, the approximates can change remarkably. The official Tabcorp totalisator fluctuations for the Carlyon Cup are shown in Table 12.9. Oval Office opened at $6.10, and weight of money saw it come in to $5.10 at the jump. When I placed my bet for the place with about 2 minutes to go he was still showing $6.10 for the win. But the interesting thing is not so much the fluctuations before they jump,

Table 12.9
Tabcorp market fluctuations for the Carlyon Cup, 1600 metres,
Caulfield, 17 February 2001

Horse	-15 min	-1 min	0 min	Final
Northerly	6.00	5.00	4.80	4.80
Oval Office	6.10	5.20	5.10	4.80
Shorblue	6.00	6.30	6.30	6.40
Furnish	22.90	22.20	22.30	21.00
Play Station	2.80	3.10	3.10	3.20
Shining Path	14.10	12.70	12.90	12.90
Iron Horse	44.40	61.50	65.50	67.30
Tiger's Eye	8.60	10.20	10.30	10.50
Collins Street	Scr	-	-	-
Kensign	31.10	40.50	43.90	44.90
Knockroe	23.60	25.50	27.20	28.20

but the change in prices after they jump. Obviously it takes the computer a few seconds to collate the approximate dividends so you never really know what you are likely to get back until about 60 seconds or more into the race. In a sprint race it can all be over before you are really sure. How much money would be needed to make Oval Office shorten 30 cents from $5.10 to $4.80 in zero seconds? A few quick calculations on the back of an envelope suggest about $5500, although it is not possible to calculate exactly because of the rounding down. This money most likely came from an arbitrageur, who bets on horses that are showing a large difference between bookmaker and totalisator prices. Oval Office started at

$4.60 for the win with the bookmakers, a 50-cent difference from the tote at the jump. The arbitrageurs used to work on the track in specially set up commission rooms, where each punter had his own operator and never faced the possibility of a lock-out in the last few seconds of betting. These days the really big arbitrageurs work from home and have their own direct line into the TAB computer. The biggest post-jump shortener of the day was Emission who came in from $4.80 at the jump to a final dividend of $4.30 in a pool of $587,625. This is equivalent to a bet of about $10,000 pinging onto the horse a millisecond before the jump.

So what does this mean for horse watchers betting at the track two minutes before the jump? Often, very little. You have to take the good with bad. The shorteners with the drifters, the nasty shocks with the most pleasant surprises. But if it is a big bet, especially for the place, and the horse is hovering around my $1.50 threshold, I'll wait until it is safely loaded in the barrier, and then try to get on in that last fraction of a millisecond.

There are many different **Betting strategies** for betting on behaviour. The totalisator pools give an indicator of the popularity of each type. In a race with a $500,000 win pool, about $250,000 will be bet on the place, $150,000 on the trifecta and $75,000 on the quinella.

Win betting is clearly the most popular, and this is how I always used to bet. A guts-and-glory punter, live and die by the sword, no wimping out with each-way or place betting. The most common win betting strategy is simply to bet on the favourite. To give you an idea of what you can expect with various win betting strategies, I sat down and queried my database. What was the likely return for a punter betting $10 for the win on the favourite in each race? The database replied that this punter had 932 bets for 281 winners, and a strike rate, you will recall, of 30.2%. The total amount outlaid was $9320 for a return of $8822, and an overall loss of $498, or -5.3%. All in all, not too bad, and a reasonable price to pay for fun and no effort. What about the favourite backer who takes a bit more trouble, looks at the favourite in the mounting yard, and only bets if the behavioural handicap is less than 20, the cut-off point? Well, things improve. This punter had 601 bets for 198 winners, a strike rate of 32.9%. The total amount outlaid was $6010 and the total returned was $6244, for a profit of $234, or 3.9%. Not too bad, really. And what about the serious fun punter, who only bets on perfect favourites with a clean sheet and no behavioural handicap? This punter had 184 bets for 64 winners, a strike rate of 34.8%. The total outlay was $1840 for a return of $2025, and a profit of $185, or 10.1%. The database reminded me that a 10% profit was sufficient for this punter to make retirement plans and book a holiday in the Grampians.

There are other alternative betting strategies for a win bettor. It could be a bet on the best selection to win (i.e. the horse with the best behavioural handicap), a bet on the long shot to win, or a bet on several horses to win using a Dutch book.

The Dutch, for some reason or another, seem to be associated with various money saving schemes. For example, there's going Dutch, or a Dutch treat, where you pay your own way. And there's the Dutch auction, where bids are reduced and not increased, and my favourite, the Dutch wife, which is a wicker frame placed between the legs for comfort whilst sleeping in the tropics! The Dutch book is a similar story, a cheapskate's betting market, reduced to just a few horses, but so that if any win, you still win. In fact, whenever I work out how much I need to outlay to win $100 on my selections I am making a Dutch book. The simplest win betting strategy and Dutch book would be to bet these various amounts on each horse for a win. Since this can often mean outlaying peculiar amounts like $46, I generally work out the bets for a total outlay of $100. Another wrinkle of a Dutch book is that I can also work it out to save on one horse, for example the favourite, and return a profit on all others. I'll show you how to do these calculations (Table 12.10).

Table 12.10
Dutch book for the Carlyon Cup, 1600 metres, Caulfield, 17 February 2001

TAB	Win dividend ($)	Bet to win $100	Bet to outlay $100	Bet to save on TAB 2 and win $100 on the rest	Bet to save on TAB 2, and outlay $100
2	5.90	17	38	6	17
3	6.10	17	37	17	50
6	14.00	8	16	8	22
11	26.80	4	9	4	11
	Outlay	46	100	35	100

The total outlay to win $100 on any of the four selections is $46. If $46 is too small a bet, simply increase the outlay by multiplying each bet by your preferred bet size, say $100, divided by the total outlay, $46. So, for example, for TAB 2, 17*(100/46) = $38. The total outlay is now 38+37+16+9 = $100.

If $46 is too much stimulation for the hip pocket nerve, it can be reduced by saving on the favourite or the shortest priced horse. In this case you would get your stake back if TAB number 2 won, and would win $100 if any of the other three horses won. You'll probably need a calculator, or the back of an envelope, to do this calculation. To save on TAB number 2:

$$\text{Saver bet} = \frac{\text{Sum of outlays on other horses}}{(\text{Saver win dividend} - 1)}$$

$$= \frac{17+8+4}{4.90}$$

$$= 5.90$$

All other bets are unchanged. The total outlay to save on the shortest price horse and win $100 on three others is now reduced to $35.

If you kinda like the idea of saving on one horse, but feel pretty loaded and would like to have a decent bet, then as before, simply multiply each bet by 100 and divide by the total outlay (here 100/35) to get the appropriate bet size.

Experienced punters, especially those furtive types in pork-pie hats with transistors glued to their ears, hate being told how to suck eggs. They will know all this stuff about Dutch books. They'll just have to keep sucking for a bit, because it can be quite fun having half the field going for you to win $100.

For multiple bettors, a box trifecta or quinella of all selections is easy and straightforward. Sophisticated trifecta bettors might like to use the best behaviour selection, or the favourite, or even the long shot, as a banker or a roving banker. A banker must finish first whereas a roving banker can finish either first, second or third. Boxes tend to get expensive over about six horses, but a banker with the rest boxed is quite affordable up to 10 horses. But my preference would be for six selections boxed with a roving banker, which gives excellent value for $90, covers seven horses, and gives the chance of a decent collect (Table 12.11). If you are ever in doubt about the costs of the various trifecta strategies you can often find the details in the race book. And in an emergency you can always ask someone with a transistor in their ear.

So, how would you go? Well, you should at least break even! And don't be depressed by that. It is an almighty accomplishment, simply to claw back the 16% take of the tote! I started out betting Dutch books on my selections, and stuck with it for over two years. I started strongly in 1998 with an average profit on turnover of 5.2%. But in 1999 I crashed to an annual profit of $22. In 2000 I took up place betting and I made just $855 for the year. In 2001 my profit on turnover started to surge higher and ended at over 11%. This year,

Table 12.11
Costs of trifecta strategies for $1

Number of selections boxed	Box all	One banker and box rest	Roving banker and box rest
3	6	6	18
4	24	12	36
5	60	20	60
6	120	30	90
7	210	42	126
8	336	56	168
9	504	72	216
10	720	90	270

2002, the Chinese Year of the Horse, I am on a streak and my profit on turnover is an outrageous and unlikely 52%. I find that I'm only having two, sometimes three bets a meeting. So, I'm betting less often, but probably outlaying more. My strike rate is currently around 60%, with an average place dividend of about $2.40. I know, I know. And The Missus keeps reminding me. I need to go out and get a decent day job!

Indeed, it remains one of life's great imponderables. That intelligent people should devote so much time and energy to racehorses and the punt for such minuscule rewards. I do it for the thrills. The adrenalin rush. I don't actually bet to win money, but to back a winner. And to have picked that winner using my own resources, what I see with my own eyes, is an electrifying feeling. I, me, I personally myself did it! No weight raters, speed handicappers, or form experts have had their way with me. I love the story of the psychologist Igor Kusyszyn, who wrote the classic paper *How gambling saved me from a misspent sabbatical*. Igor spent his study leave from the university gambling - playing the horses, cards and blackjack - and in between times he interviewed real gamblers. He concluded that gambling was an expression of the need to search for meaning in life:

> a need that may be so powerful, pressing so hard for fulfillment, that the individual is willing to suffer financial loss, social isolation, and even personal tragedy in responding to it.

Gambling confirms our existence and our self worth. Gambling confirms that we are alive.

I love too the apocryphal story of the sociologist approaching the winning punter who has just had a huge collect. The sociologist asked the punter how he picked the winner. Replied the punter: "Who do you think I am, a nobody?"

Chapter 13 Which horse, which race?

Not all horses and not all races are the same. For starters, there are blacks, greys, chestnuts, bays and browns. There are fillies and colts, mares, geldings and stallions. There are low class races restricted to horses who have never won a race, and high class races, like the weight-for-age Cox Plate. There are helter-skelter sprints like the Oakleigh Plate, and endurance tests like the Melbourne Cup. With so much variability it seems quite possible that horse watchers might find it easier to put the pencil through horses in some races than in others.

This is an excellent question, sorry query, for my database. So I asked it: "What are the behavioural handicaps for each different class of race?" Figure 13.1 shows the reply and gives the average behavioural handicaps for all horses in each class of race and also for the winners. The best-behaved horses were clearly the two-year-olds. This is most interesting as it suggests that these green horses haven't yet learnt or started to display the bad behaviour of older open class horses. When I first started watching horses I didn't even bother to look at the early two-year-old races, mainly because I accepted the conventional wisdom that these horses were too green and erratic. However, I have now found that it is in these races of untried horses that I have most success. A two-year-old racing with no behavioural handicap has a tremendous advantage if the rest of the field are losing their heads.

The best races for a horse watcher to bet on will be those where the winner can be easily and clearly distinguished from the rest of the field. So, these are the races in Figure 13.1 in which the behavioural handicaps of the winners (black bars) are significantly less than all horses (grey bars). Weight-for-age races are obviously a terrific

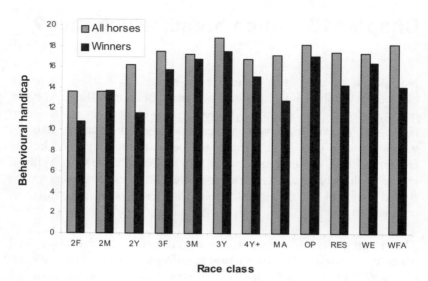

Race class

Key to race classes:

2F	Two-years-old fillies
2M	Two-years-old colts and geldings
2Y	Two-years-old
3F	Three-years-old fillies
3M	Three-years-old colts and geldings
3Y	Three-years-old
4Y+	Four-years-old and over
MA	Mares
OP	Open handicap
RES	Restricted race with special conditions, e.g. one metropolitan win in the last year
WE	Welter handicap
WFA	Weight for age

Figure 13.1
Average behavioural handicaps by race class.

betting opportunity, as are Restricted races, Mares, Two-years-old, and Two-years-old fillies.

I enjoy betting on two-year-old and three-year-old fillies races, generally because the winner is easier to distinguish from other horses, but also because I don't have to contend with the problem of young male horses feeling their oats. This behaviour is generally described by horse people as "coltish" - the horse is headstrong, aggressive, dominant, and difficult to handle. An example is Bel Esprit, the favourite and winner of the 2002 Blue Diamond. The horse refused to enter the barrier and in any other race probably would have been scratched. The trainer described Bel Esprit's antics as "playful". However, a stallion chain was required to control the horse at his next start in the Golden Slipper. There is no doubt that these strong, dominant horses can win races. And also, there is no doubt that strong, dominant behaviour can interfere with race performance. Horse watchers need to take extra care with races for two- and three-year-old colts and geldings. Strong, dominant behaviour can also interfere with the interpretation of behavioural handicaps.

I also asked my database: "What are the behavioural handicaps for each different race distance?" The reply is shown in Figure 13.2. Clearly, the best races will be sprint races over 1000 to 1200 metres and middle distance races over 1300 to 1600 metres. As the distance increases above 1600 metres the winners tend to look much like all the other horses.

So, in summary, my favourite races are Two-years-old fillies, Two-years-old, Mares and Weight-for-age, up to about 1600 metres. I used to shy away from 1000 metre sprint races because I thought if something went wrong the horse had no time to recover, no matter how well behaved it was. I now realise that things are likely to go wrong if the horse has a bad behavioural handicap. Because I feel I have an advantage in Fillies and Mares races I tend to bet more in these races than I would in other races. Someone, somewhere, once

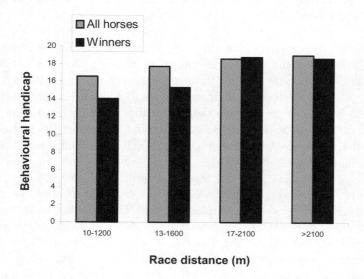

Figure 13.2
Average behavioural handicaps by race distance.

said that it "takes courage to be a pig". I believe this wholeheartedly, and try to act upon it. When I have a tremendous conviction about a standout selection in one of these races I normally go for glory and double my bet.

I might also bet more if a horse shows a sudden improvement in behaviour. I quickly get to know the fractious horses and any change in behaviour is usually immediately obvious. Consider the headstrong former West Australian mare, Voile D'Or (Table 13.1). This mare had a clear attitude problem for many weeks, culminating in a behavioural handicap of 129% on Oaks Day, 9 November 2000. A certain loser. Two starts later at Moonee Valley she wasn't even pawing in the birdcage, and only showed a very brief head up in the

Table 13.1
Behaviour of the mare Voile D'Or over seven successive starts

Date	Birdcage	Ring	Yard	Track	Behaviour handicap	Place
30 Sep	Paw		Two hands Slope Change gait Fast Head up Buck	Clerk	84	13
14 Oct	Paw		Two hands Circle Buck Head up		76	10
21 Oct	Paw Pony		Baulk Two hands Change gait Head up Snort		46	16
9 Nov	Paw Weave Nibble No strapper Neigh	Salivate Loll	Two hands Head up Change gait Circle Snort	Resist	129	15
25 Nov	Paw		Two hands Circle Fast Head out	Sweat 3	71	12
9 Dec			Head up Snort		4	1
16 Dec	Paw			Sweat 1 Head up Clerk	18	3

mounting yard. She powered away to a terrific victory. At her next start at Flemington she was also well behaved, although I noticed the clerk holding her with the jockey dismounted and standing on the track. She finished third. Quite clearly, horses can show signs of when they are less likely to lose!

Horses can also show signs of when they have had enough racing. Consider another of my favourite mares, Heart of Egypt. When I backed her for a place at Caulfield on 14 October 2000, I could find no fault (*see* Chapter 1, page 12). It was her fifth start since 12 July and she ran a great third. She then raced extremely consistently over the spring and early summer, and by the time she raced again at Caulfield on Blue Diamond Stakes day on 24 February 2001 she had racked up 13 starts in just over seven months, having a run on average every 17 days. She had also racked up the impressive record of seven placings, including one win, in this long campaign. When I saw her on Blue Diamond day she was pawing as usual in her stall, but baulked on entering the mounting yard. Her ears were to the side and flicking, her head was up and she was sweating slightly. Her head remained up with the jockey up. With some emotion I put the pen through her. It had been a very long spring. She finished fourth of the six runners.

Overtraining is a well-known phenomenon in human athletes, and is associated with feelings of fatigue, poor performance and physiological and psychological changes. A similar phenomenon probably occurs in horses, and recently has been investigated by Catherine Tyler-McGowan and her colleagues at the University of Sydney. Catherine was looking for a physiological marker of overtraining, a blood chemical that could be used to provide an early warning. She measured many variables, including feed intake, bodyweight, various blood chemicals and the time to fatigue on a treadmill in a standard exercise test. Overtrained horses were exercised at greater intensities, more often and for a longer time than control horses. Catherine found that the overtrained horses lost bodyweight and fatigued more rapidly, but there were no consistent changes in the various blood parameters that could be used as an indicator of overtraining. However, of great interest to horse watchers were the marked changes observed in the behaviour patterns of the overtrained group of horses. Some horses showed headstrong behaviour or were fractious, others were reluctant to get onto the treadmill, suffered interference injuries, or tossed their heads about when the gas mask was put in place. Some simply stopped or refused to continue on the treadmill before the finish of training. One horse pawed the treadmill. Quite clearly, horses can show through their behaviour when they have had enough.

Horses may also show signs of imminent injury. Consider Black Bean, a striking horse. He was the sort of horse that I could never cross out. Invariably he rocked up to the yard with a ring bit and a stiff tail. Sometimes he might be chewing slightly on the bit, sometimes salivating slightly, but always well behaved. At Moonee Valley on 23 March 2002 he appeared in the parade ring for the Australia Stakes with his head up, salivating and gaping. But what really put the wind up me was that he was clacking, or striking himself. He was the first horse that I crossed out. This had never, ever happened before. Black Bean, the magnificent beast, broke down during the running of the race and was destroyed. It gave me goose bumps.

Horses also have very good memories, especially of aversive events. Consider Mister Obliging, at Caulfield on 2 March 2002. His gait was not just slow, but painfully slow, repeatedly baulking and propping on his way up to the mounting yard. There was no way he was going to walk into that mounting yard. He just did not want to be there. As the immortal Bert Bryant would say, only a spendthrift with a sense of humour would want to back him. To understand this behaviour you needed to have witnessed his run at Caulfield the previous Saturday, when he was accidentally struck on the face by the whip of another jockey. This sort of information is usually available in the *Stewards' Reports* on the Internet, although I had seen Mister Obliging struck at first hand. Mister Obliging ran equal fourth, which was a remarkable effort considering his mental attitude to racing that day.

The *Stewards' Reports* contain a lot of information that can help explain a horse's failure. There are generally detailed explanations of which horses were tightened for room, inconvenienced, or held up for a run. I have no particular interest in these explanations, unless I come across a really good excuse which is not covered in my Top 50 (*see* Chapter 5). Sometimes I am interested in a horse that "threw its head in the air, and raced ungenerously when being restrained", but only to confirm that my pre-race predictions of unruly behaviour were accurate. Consider, Mystic Melody at Moonee Valley on 27 April 2002. Her race book entry was: Neck twisted, Gaping, Tongue tie, Lolling, Baulking, Tugging, Ears back, Sweating. The *Stewards' Report* noted:

> Mystic Melody refused to jump with the field when the gates were released, and took no part in the race. The trainer of Mystic Melody, was notified that the mare was suspended from racing until such time as it performs to the satisfaction of the Stewards in a trial.

I am more interested in horses in the *Stewards' Reports* where a veterinary examination revealed that the horse was sore or lame in a fore or hind leg, or short in its action. I check these horses against my race book to see if I observed anything unusual in the pre-race gait. And, I am most interested in anything that might have happened during the running of the race which could affect a horse's mental attitude at its next start. So I take note of remarks such as:

- brushed the running rail
- became cast in the barrier
- was showing signs of distress with an elevated heart beat
- had a haematoma on its near shoulder
- was galloped on, on both hind legs
- was distressed and showing signs of a respiratory complaint
- reared over at the barrier
- was kicked by another runner at the barrier
- the rider was fined for excessive use of the whip.

I generally record these horses in my Black Book. Black Books can be tricky things. My view is that they are OK for recording Black Marks against a horse's name, but I have found them less useful for recording positives. Every now and then I become totally besotted with particular horses. These horses are often mares, and if they appeared as a standout selection in the mounting yard and ran accordingly I used to stick them in my Black Book. Once in the Black Book I would bet on them for the next two starts, regardless. But these horses can often let you down. Commands went into the Black Book after appearing as a standout in the 1999 Caulfield Guineas (*see* page 6). But he was tipped out straight away at his next start, without even a bet, when he turned up for the Cox Plate sporting a brand new nose roll. Commands hated it and was doing everything in his power to toss it off his head. No wonder he ran off the track! Black Books can cause much grief. Each race throws up different forces and interactions between horses which can influence outcomes. I find it easier and simpler to start with a clean sheet and not have history hanging over my head. Throwing away the form guide gives me a sense of total freedom. And it is the same with behavioural handicaps. Without the burden of past appearances and Black Books I can look at each horse and bet on it according to its merits on the day. So my Black Book is exactly that - a book of Black Marks from the past, and with no imperatives for the future. And I suppose that is my philosophy of gambling. To live for the day, the adrenalin rush, of picking and backing a winner. To be unfettered by form. To be free of the past and not constrained by the future. To ignore all tipsters, touts, lairs, urgers and coat-tuggers. To bet on what I see. For sensation seekers, fun lovers and partygoers, this has to be the way.

And the future? I am told that in Hong Kong they have stands around the mounting yard that hold thousands of people. These are the prized seats on the track, and there is keen interest in looking at the horses. If I leave Melbourne, I seldom venture further than the Grampians, so I can't confirm these reports. But there seems little doubt that watching racehorses is more life affirming than watching spinning reels or the fall of the cards. Maybe we'll see vast stands around our own mounting yards. After all, you can see some amazing scenes. There's not much to surpass the sight of John Singleton astride his wife, celebrating the win of Ha Ha in the 2001 Slipper (Photo 58).

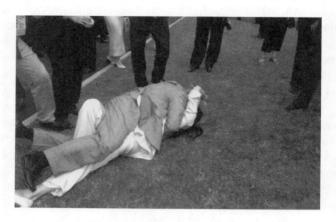

Photo 58
John Singleton and wife in mounting yard
(photograph by Barry Chapman and reproduced courtesy of *The Age*).

The future. It's scary, really. There is no doubt that the information contained in this book is going to bring about great change. Indeed, a sea change. The strike rate of favourites, which has remained immutable at 30% for centuries, could creep up towards 35%. The dividends on favourites with perfect behavioural handicaps will certainly fall. Racetrack attendances will increase when the advantages of horse watching become evident to the ordinary punter. Race clubs may even attempt to ban the use of mobile phones at the track - not to prevent communication of odds, but communication of behavioural handicaps. Even clipboards could disappear! Smart punters will be armed with a Palm Pilot for scoring behaviour. The Pilot will be programmed with an advanced mathematical model of bad behaviour and will transmit the selections to a computer at home.

This computer will compare prices in Melbourne, Sydney, Darwin, Vanuatu and Gibraltar, and automatically make the bet at the best price available online.

I don't think I like change. I'm always afraid that technology might leave me behind. I carry my list of 65 variables around in my head. But for apprentice horse watchers this might be a bit daunting, so I have made up a simplified cheat sheet of bad behaviour in Table 13.2. It's probably worthwhile making a single photocopy of this page for the purposes of private study, and using it as a bookmark in your race book. I simply hope that I can go on using my trusty pen and my trusty necktop computer for a while yet. Thank goodness the only technology problem I have at the moment is with data entry. Sometimes I have trouble reading my own writing.

Table 13.2
Cheat sheet

© Geoffrey Hutson 2002

Location	Variable	Behavioural handicap
Birdcage	Pawing	-10
	Weaving	-41
	Kicking	-26
	No strapper	-13
	Hand-held	-4
Ring	Neck twisted	-15
	Gaping	-22
	Tongue tie	-7
	Crossover noseband	-43
	Nose roll	-14
	Pacifiers	-8
	White eye	-4
	Cannon bandages	-17
	Other bandages	-70
Yard	Two strappers	-6
	Baulking	-18
	Two hands	-10
	Circling	-26
	Strapper remarks	-12
	Slow gait	-40
	Fast gait	-25
	Changing gait	-4
	Bucking	-26
	Head up	-4
	Ears side or back	-8
	Ears flicking	-4
	Dumping	-8
	Sex signs	-15
Track	Overweight jockey	-40
	Head up - jockey up	-3
	Grabbed by clerk	-5
	Late	-41
	Resisting	-21

Chapter 14 The Melbourne Cup

The Melbourne Cup is a horse watcher's nightmare. I used to pretend that it didn't exist, that it wasn't a race for serious fun punters. The trouble is, it doesn't go away. And it's getting bigger. If the whole nation stops, then you feel that maybe you should stop too. And you have no street cred unless you can pick the winner. I'm afraid my credibility is in tatters. I have had two winners in over 30 years. Arwon in 1978, and everyone's favourite, Subzero in 1992. You'd think that since I wised up to horse behaviour that my strike rate would have improved. Well, maybe it's something to do with my star sign. I'm a Hiraji. 1947. Number 12, a four-year-old grey gelding, J. Purtell, red and white check, red cap, barrier 11, SP 12/1. What are you?

1997

From rooster to feather duster. Last year I was famous, besieged by the media, strutting around as if I owned the barnyard. This year I'm low profile, having a bet, and in love with Ebony Grosve. He was my long-range tip after the Derby last year. Looked beautiful before the Mackinnon, nice and relaxed.

In the birdcage Ebony Grosve has a heap of people around his stall, many laughing. The horse is performing the flehmen or lip curl, where the teeth are exposed and the top lip curled way back (*see* Chapter 8, page 113). It's an unusual behaviour pattern, shown mainly by stallions, and could indicate the presence of a filly or mare on heat. I quickly check the horse in the adjacent stall - a three-year-old filly. This is not a good sign.

When they come into the parade ring Ebony Grosve is back to his usual calm self. But the band of Scottish pipers is marching down the straight, and as they get closer the drumbeats start to unsettle a lot of the horses. Ebony hates it. Starts rearing, eyes bulging, whirling his tail, head up. Suddenly, all hell breaks loose and The Roulettes scream overhead. "Vroooooooooom". He doesn't like that at all. He props, strapper tugging with full force on the strap, and refuses to enter the laneway. Then he starts squealing, squealing. I can't remember the last time I heard a horse squeal at the track. It's absolutely awful. My Cup bet is history! I can't back Might and Power because he behaves like a potential puller, all reefing and tearing, and so, with little zest, I back a few others. They lose. I trudge home, and don't even have a beer. There's always next year.

Feather duster? I get home to find a letter from the Pig Research and Development Corporation. The grant for my research project is to be terminated on December 31 and the provisional patent on my invention, the "Rootin' Tootin' pig feeder", will be allowed to lapse. Sacked! Unemployed at 50! It's a hard life being a behaviour researcher, both at work and play.

1998

It's 1.30 pm on Cup Day, and I'm sitting on my favourite seat in the birdcage. Frankie Dettori has just walked past, Brylcreemed up, oozing with confidence. But I think I have a problem. A strategic problem. I normally look at the horses and then bet in the two minutes before they jump. Today there are 100,606 other punters trying to do the same thing. So I work it out backwards. The Cup starts at 3.20, so I'll need to secure my position on the parade ring corner at 2.20. That means I'll need to line up for my beer at 2.00, and line up for my bet at 1.40, and line up for my leak on the grey slates at 1.30. Hey, time to go!

It's 2.05 and I haven't got my bet on. The machine has broken down. A harried, red-faced techo coaxes it back to life. I'm very toey. At last I'm on. A big bet on Champagne, on the nose. 2.25 and I'm in the best spot on the course, on the corner of the parade ring where it joins the race leading to the mounting yard. No horse can get past me! Some Cup horses are walking around, anonymous to most of the crowd. There's one that's at least 17 hands. Gosh! Must be Persian Punch. Clipped, but with a patch of northern hemisphere coat left on the back. Looks most excellent. You'd have to say it, very impressive. The strapper is getting irritated with Taufan's Melody. Looks a lot crankier today, tossing his head about, and a bit distracted by the crowd. A tough old nut, though. Doriemus, same age, always looks the same, but this year perhaps a bit underweight. Trainers, owners, saddles, and bigwigs arrive. First out is Peak of Perfection, dragging the strapper behind him. He's got funny polystyrene protectors on his bumpers. I'm surprised he's allowed to get away with that, since bandages need to be sewn, and these things look like they could fly off during the race. More stewards' discretion to the OS brigade, I suppose. Second out, Taufan's Melody. Then a heap of them. Faithful Son looks OK, but is still a very light type with heavy bandages. Lots of nose rolls today. Count Chivas, Darazari, Sheer Danzig, Second Coming. Yorkshire, a head up horse, is also sweating up a bit. A flighty type, I think. Markham, perfect. The Hind has a one-eyed blinker (they are desperate) and is also sweating up. Three Crowns' strapper needs help from a security guard to hold him, and also sports the polystyrene protectors. Yippyio is sweating. Tie The Knot has his ears back and, to this watcher, seems to be in a sour mood. Gold Guru is aroused. Skybeau is lolling his tongue around. Ancient City is long odds. Perpetual Check also has his ears back, but is OK. Champagne looks perfect. Aerosmith, not as good as at Caulfield. Chewing ferociously on the bit, the strapper tugging on the strap. Jezabeel. Wow. Have I seen this horse before? Relaxed, beautiful coat, a backside like a barn door. I can't remember how I scored her in the Caulfield Cup. Wish I had my race book. They're going up. Where's the three year old? Last out, Arena. Looks great. I've got to have some savers! A dash to the tote, and there's only 10 ahead of me, not many hats. I save on Persian Punch, Markham, Jezabeel and Arena.

They're off! And Gold Guru, as you could predict, is leading them. Arena and Jezabeel are in nice possies. Home turn, and runs galore. Persian Punch! The clocktower. Champagne is storming for the line. She's half a length in front. I'm rich, rich. What will I have? Krug? Moet? Jezabeel! How is it possible? Taufan's Melody fourth. Nice run, tough nut, beaten by the handicapper.

Home on the courtesy bus to Epsom Road. The bus is full of drunk transvestites. Ugly! My fashion prizes? A tie between the 50 Flintstones cavorting on the sand track and the Thomas The Tank Engine 4WD. I can't wait to get home and check my Caulfield Cup race book. There it is. Jezabeel was perfect then, too. Oh well, at least I didn't lose. And there's always next year.

1999

Things are going to be different this year. For starters, I don't even need to look at Rogan Josh. I know I won't be backing him. I know he's a Cummings' horse, but he's not a typical Cummings. Not relaxed like Saintly. The curry is always fired up. He was sweating a bit before the Caulfield Cup, grinding on the bit. In the Mackinnon he was head up, short stride, with a sloping strapper. I know he won, but I can't have him. Today he's the same. Head up, sweating, sloping strapper, short stride.

I have no particular memory of what won The Cup this year. But I do know for sure, there's always another year.

2000

The weather forecast is windy, with a flying millinery warning. Normally I'd sit up and take notice, but I don't care. I've got a pain in my head, in my left brain ventricle, all the way along. The *Reader's Digest Australian Family Medical Adviser* is not much help. The Symptom Sorter reckons I've just got a tension headache, and that there's no need to consult the doctor. But it makes me worried about my health. The Missus says women have them all the time, and live with them, and that I should stop whingeing. I was born a hypochondriac. It's hard to stop. I would if the pain would.

A mob of boys in black suits and black ties descends on our place for croissants and Baileys before heading off with my daughter K8 and her friend Honor Bradbeer in smart red hats. Where are the gorilla suits? What's happening to The Cup?

I slowly crank up and check out the brother-in-law, property developer and real estate tycoon, in his stall in the Birdcage on the Rails. It is a peculiar phenomenon this, where the members install themselves in stalls and the uninstalled members walk past inspecting the flesh. Just like I do with the horses. He enjoys introducing me as a horse psychologist.

I walk out to The Lawn, but 121,015 people means that it is futile to even attempt to find two red hats and a few black suits. So I sit in the stand, close my eyes with the throbbing pain, and whinge quietly to myself. At 2.20 I grab a spot on the mounting yard rail and wait. This is my first year as a member and I'm pretty pleased to secure such a prime position. I narrow them down to three horses, Freemason, Lightning Arrow and Brew. I'm shocked that I can actually walk into the tote hall and get a bet on. I back the first two for a place. Brew wins. My headache seems to be thumping, harder. Who can I whinge to? How could there possibly be another year?

2001

Well, it's wet this year. Very, very soggy. Not a good day for the high-heeled penetrometers. You could fire a cannon down the Members' Lawn and not score a single socialite (Photo 59). So it's a free bet. Horses can have the best behavioural handicap in the world, but it still doesn't help them pick their feet up in the wet. I don't bet in the wet. Except for The Cup.

Photo 59
Members' Lawn, Cup Day, 2001.

A free bet. I don't like the Caulfield Cup winner, Ethereal, though. A real Jekyll-and-Hyde of a horse. In the birdcage the most beautifully serene and calm horse you could ever see, surrounded by teams of doting women strappers, attending to every possible equine whim. In the mounting yard, a horse possessed, in urgent need of The Exorcist. Two, or is it three, strappers? Head up, circling, wheeling, turning, goose stepping, and stomping on Sheila Laxon's mobile. I suppose you could be kind and say - keen.

I go for a place bet on the iron horse. The big, old, reliable, courageous, magnificent, relaxed English stayer, Persian Punch. Will grind it out, has been here before, loves the distance, and most importantly, revels in the wet.

$5.20 for third. Is there any street cred for third?

Further reading

Introduction

Beyer, A. (1993). Beyer on Speed. Houghton Mifflin Company, New York.

Scott, D. (1978). Winning. Puntwin, Sydney.

Plante, R. and Plante, M. (1974). Australian Horse Racing and Punter's Guide. Rem and Marcel Plante, Sydney.

Chapter 2

Carroll, C.L. and Huntington, P.J. (1988). Body condition scoring and weight estimation of horses. Equine Veterinary Journal 20, 41-45.

Ellis, P. (2000). Condition scoring and weight estimation of horses. Agricuture Note AG0928, Department of Natural Resources and Environment, Victoria. Internet: www.nre.vic.gov.au - search *condition scoring*.

Evans, D.L. (2000). Training and Fitness in Athletic Horses. Rural Industries Research and Development Corporation, Barton, ACT. Internet: www.rirdc.gov.au/reports/HOR/00-01.pdf

Henneke, D.R. (1985). A condition score system for horses. Equine Practice 7(9): 13-15.

Chapter 3

Hutson, G.D. and Haskell, M.J. (1997). Pre-race behaviour of horses as a predictor of race finishing order. Applied Animal Behaviour Science 53, 231-248.

Snyder, W.W. (1978). Horse racing: testing the efficient markets model. Journal of Finance 33, 1109-1118.

Chapter 4

Anderson, I. (1996). Losers show their colours at the starting gate. New Scientist 152 (2054), 7.

Anonymous (1996). Look of a loser leads to the winning pick. University of Melbourne UniNews 5(43), 1. Internet: www.unimelb.edu.au/ExtRels/Media/UN/archive/1996/143/lo okofaloserleadstothewinn.html

Chapter 5

Morris, D. (1988). Horsewatching. Crown Publishers, New York.

Chapter 6

Cooper, J.J., McDonald, L. and Mills, D.S. (2000). The effect of increasing visual horizons on stereotypic weaving: implications for the social housing of stabled horses. Applied Animal Behaviour Science 69, 67-83.

Crawley, J. and Chamove, A.S. (1997). Thoroughbred race horse behavioural responses to human contact. Proceedings Annual Conference New Zealand Psychological Society. Edited by G.M. Habermann, pp. 16-21.

Feh, C. and de Mazières, J. (1993). Grooming at a preferred site reduces heart rate in horses. Animal Behaviour 46, 1191-1194.

Lagerweij, E., Nelis, P.C., Wiegant, V.M. and van Ree, J.M. (1984). The twitch in horses: a variant of acupuncture. Science 225, 1172-1174.

Lynch, J.J., Fregin, G.F., Mackie, J.B. and Monroe, R.R. (1974). Heart rate changes in the horse to human contact. Psychophysiology 11, 472-478.

McGreevy, P. (1996). Why Does My Horse...? Souvenir Press, London.

Ödberg, F.O. (1973). An interpretation of pawing by the horse (*Equus caballus* Linnaeus), displacement activity and original functions. Säugetierkundliche Mitteilungen 40, 1-12.

Chapter 7

Anthony, D., Telegin, D.Y. and Brown, D. (1991). The origin of horseback riding. Scientific American, December, 44-48A.

Barker, R. (1990). The mind behind the swirls. Rocky Mountain Quarter Horse 28 (March), 26-27.

Bowers, J.R. and Slocombe, R.F. (1999). Influence of girth strap tensions on athletic performance of racehorses. Equine Exercise Physiology 5. Equine Veterinary Journal, Supplement 30, 52-56.

Bowers, J. and Slocombe, R. (2000). Tensions used on girths on Thoroughbred racehorses. Australian Veterinary Journal 78, 567-569.

Grandin, T., Deesing, M.J., Struthers, J.J. and Swinker, A.M. (1995). Cattle with hair whorl patterns above the eyes are more behaviorally agitated during restraint. Applied Animal Behaviour Science 46, 117-123.

Keegan, K.G., Baker, G.J., Boero, M.J., Pijanowski, G.J. and Phillips, J.W. (1992). Evaluation of support bandaging during measurement of proximal sesamoidean ligament strain in horses by use of a mercury strain gauge. American Journal of Veterinary Research 53, 1203-1208.

Morlock, M.M., Kobluk, C.N., Jones, J.H., Rolsten, G.K. and Faass, J.K. (1994). Influence of bandage material on pressure distribution under the bandage on the distal forelimb of the galloping horse. Gait & Posture 2, 253-260.

Roberts, T. (1985). Horse Control and the Bit. T.A. and P.R. Roberts, 241 West Beach Road, Richmond, South Australia, 5033.

Victoria Racing Club (2000). Rules of Racing. Contains Australian and Local Rules of Racing, Rules of Betting and Regulations. Racing Victoria Centre, 400 Epsom Road, Flemington, 3031.

Westervelt, R.G., Stouffer, J.R., Hintz, H.F. and Schryver, H.F. (1976). Estimating fatness in horses and ponies. Journal of Animal Science 43, 781-785.

Wright, I.M. (1987). Equipment for the care, protection and restraint of horses. In: Horse Management, 2nd Edition. Edited by J. Hickman, Academic Press, London, pp. 203-244.

Chapter 8

Argo, C.McG., Collingsworth, M.G.R. and Cox, J.E. (2001). Seasonal changes in reproductive and pelage status during the initial 'quiescent' and first 'active' breeding seasons of the peripubertal pony colt. Animal Science 72, 55-64.

Australian Stud Book (2000). Australian Jockey Club, Randwick, Sydney. Internet: www.studbook.aust.com

Byers, S.W., Dowsett, K.F. and Glover, T.D. (1983). Seasonal and circadian changes of testosterone levels in the peripheral blood plasma of stallions and their relation to semen quality. Journal of Endocrinology 99, 141-150.

Citron, N.D. and Wade, P.J. (1980). Penile injuries from vacuum cleaners. British Medical Journal 281, 26.

Dowsett, K.F. (1982). The breeding season and semen characteristics. Journal of Reproduction and Fertility, Supplement 32, 636-637.

Dowsett, K.F., Knott, L.M., Woodward, R.A. and Bodero, D.A.V. (1993). Seasonal variation in the estrous cycle of mares in the subtropics. Theriogenology 39, 651-653.

Lindsay, F.E.F. and Burton, F.L. (1983). Observational study of "urine testing" in the horse and donkey stallion. Equine Veterinary Journal 15, 330-336.

Line, S.W., Hart, B.L. and Sanders, L. (1985). Effect of prepubertal versus postpubertal castration on sexual and aggressive behavior in male horses. Journal of the American Veterinary Medical Association 186, 249-251.

McCall, C.A. (1991). Utilizing taped stallion vocalizations as a practical aid in estrus detection in mares. Applied Animal Behaviour Science 28, 305-310.

McDonnell, S.M. (1988). Spontaneous erection and masturbation in Equids. In: Proceedings 35th Annual Meeting of Association of Equine Practitioners, Boston, MA, pp. 567-580.

McDonnell, S.M. (1992). Normal and abnormal sexual behaviour. Veterinary Clinics of North America: Equine Practice 8, 71-89.

Osborne, V.E. (1966). An analysis of the pattern of ovulation as it occurs in the annual reproductive cycle of the mare in Australia. Australian Veterinary Journal 42, 149-154.

Tischner, M. (1982). Patterns of stallion sexual behaviour in the absence of mares. Journal of Reproduction and Fertility, Supplement 32, 65-70.

Tyler, S.J. (1972). The behaviour and social organization of the New Forest ponies. Animal Behaviour Monographs 5, 87-196.

Chapter 9

Bailey, C.J., Reid, S.W.J., Hodgson, D.R. and Rose, R.J. (1999). Impact of injuries and disease on a cohort of two- and three-year-old thoroughbreds in training. Veterinary Record 145, 487-493.

Budiansky, S. (1997). The Nature of Horses. Orion Books, London.

Butler, D. (1998). Hoof soundness evaluation techniques. In: Farriery, a Convention for Farriers and Veterinarians, Postgraduate Foundation in Veterinary Science, University of Sydney, pp. 57-65.

Cohen, N.D., Mundy, G.D., Peloso, J.G., Carey, V.J. and Amend, N.K. (1999). Results of physical inspection before races and race-related characteristics and their association with musculoskeletal injuries in Thoroughbreds during races. Journal of the American Veterinary Medical Association 215, 654-661.

Cook, W.R. (1998). Use of the bit in horses. Veterinary Record 142, 200.

Fraser, A.F. (1992). The Behaviour of the Horse. CAB International, Wallingford, Oxon.

Griffiths, J.B., Steel, C.M., Symons, P.J. and Yovich, J.V. (2000). Improving the predictability of performance by prerace detection of dorsal metacarpal disease in Thoroughbred racehorses. Australian Veterinary Journal 78, 466-467.

Harman, A.S., Moore, S., Hoskins, R. and Keller, P. (1999). Horse vision and an explanation for the visual behaviour originally explained by the 'ramp retina'. Equine Veterinary Journal 31, 384-390.

Holmström, M. (2001). The effects of conformation. In: Equine Locomotion. Edited by W. Back and H.M. Clayton, W.B. Saunders, London, pp. 281-295.

Kiley, M. (1972). The vocalizations of ungulates, their causation and function. Zeitschrift für Tierpsychologie 31, 171-222.

Kiley-Worthington, M. (1975). The tail movements of ungulates, canids and felids, with particular reference to their causation and function as displays. Behaviour 56, 69-115.

Kiley-Worthington, M. (1987). The Behaviour of Horses in Relation to Management and Training. J.A. Allen, London.

Kriz, N.G., Hodgson, D.R. and Rose, R.J. (2000). Prevalence and clinical importance of heart murmurs in racehorses. Journal of the American Veterinary Medical Association 216, 1441-1445.

McClure, S.R., Glickman, L.T. and Glickman, N.W. (1999). Prevalence of gastric ulcers in show horses. Journal of the American Veterinary Medical Association 215, 1130-1133.

Mordin, N. (1994). The Winning Look. Aesculus Press, Oswestry, Shropshire.

Takach, J. (1993). Postures, Profiles and Performance. Spiral bound manuscript, 139 pp., available from the Gambler's Bookshop, 630 South 11th Street, Las Vegas NV 89101, USA.

Waring, G.H. (1983). Horse Behavior. Noyes Publications, Park Ridge, New Jersey, USA.

Weeks, J. and Beck, A.M. (1996). Equine agitation behaviors. Equine Practice 18(6), 23-24.
Young, Alan and Burt, Bill (1994). Mister Ed and Me. St. Martin's Press, New York.

Chapter 10

Beeley, J.G., Eason, R. and Snow, D.H. (1986). Isolation and characterization of latherin, a surface-active protein from horse sweat. Biochemical Journal 235, 645-650.
Hodgson, D.R., Davis, R.E. and McConaghy, F.F. (1994). Thermoregulation in the horse in response to exercise. British Veterinary Journal 150, 219-235.
McCutcheon, L.J., Geor, R.J., Ecker, G.L. and Lindinger, M.I. (1999). Equine sweating responses to submaximal exercise during 21 days of heat acclimation. Journal of Applied Physiology 87, 1843-1851.
Tyler, C.M., Hodgson, D.R. and Rose, R.J. (1996). Effect of a warm-up on energy supply during high intensity exercise in horses. Equine Veterinary Journal 28, 117-120.

Chapter 12

Ainslie, T. and Ledbetter, B. (1980). The Body Language of Horses. William Morrow and Co., New York.
Aitken, A. (1997). Hats in the Ring. Harper Collins Publishers, Sydney.
Conlon, B. (1997). Totalisator history.
    Internet: www.ozemail.com.au/~bconlon
Eddy, A. (2002). Bookmaker fined for fake bets on the "Card". The Age, 5 February.
Kusyszyn, I. (1977). How gambling saved me from a misspent sabbatical. Journal of Humanistic Psychology 17 (3), 19-34.
Pain, S. (2000). Odds on winner. New Scientist, 27 May, 44-45.

Waterhouse, R. (1993). Fine Cotton, fine scandal: unmasking an infamous substitution. Australian Cultural History 12, 52-67.

Chapter 13

Racing Services Bureau (2002). Stewards' Reports - Victorian Racing. Internet: www.racingvictoria.net.au/rsb/steward.htm

Tyler-McGowan, C.M., Golland, L.C., Evans, D.L., Hodgson, D.R. and Rose, R.J. (1999). Haematological and biochemical responses to training and overtraining. Equine Exercise Physiology 5. Equine Veterinary Journal, Supplement 30, 621-625.

Chapter 14

Reader's Digest (1984). Australian Family Medical Adviser. Reader's Digest, Sydney.

Index